FINDING
CHRIST WITHIN

IRMA ZALESKI

FINDING
CHRIST WITHIN

NOVALIS

© 2007 Novalis, Saint Paul University, Ottawa, Canada

Cover design and layout: Dominique Pelland
Cover image: © Lynne McIlvride Evans

Business Offices:
Novalis Publishing Inc.
10 Lower Spadina Avenue, Suite 400
Toronto, Ontario, Canada
M5V 2Z2

Novalis Publishing Inc.
4475 Frontenac Street
Montréal, Québec, Canada
H2H 2S2

Phone: 1-800-387-7164
Fax: 1-800-204-4140
E-mail: books@novalis.ca
www.novalis.ca

Library and Archives Canada Cataloguing in Publication

Zaleski, Irma
    Finding Christ within / Irma Zaleski.

ISBN 978-2-89507-838-8

    1. Christian life. I. Title.

BV4501.3.Z35 2007   248.4   C2007-900282-X

Printed in Canada.

Scripture quotations are taken from the New American Bible (Oxford: Oxford University Press, 1990).

We acknowledge the financial support of the Government of Canada through the Book Publishing Industry Development Program (BPIDP) for our publishing activities.

5   4   3   2   1   11   10   09   08   07

CONTENTS

INTRODUCTION

During a visit to England 30 or 35 years ago, while browsing in a London bookshop, I picked up a little blue book called *Christ Within*. I am not sure what drew my attention to it: perhaps its size—like a small, thin prayer book—or the fact that it was written by an anonymous author, or simply because its title aroused my curiosity.

Whatever the reason, I bought the book, and over the next few weeks and months I read it many times. Eventually, however, I put it aside. I did not think of it again until a few years ago when, in connection with something I was working on, I looked for it among my books. It was not there. I must have lent it to somebody or given it away.

I tried to locate another copy. I went to various bookstores and had a search done on the Internet, but could not find it anywhere. I even contacted the bookshop where I had originally bought it, but was told that there was no record of having had such a book in stock. I think they suspected that I had imagined the whole thing. But I knew I had not. I remembered it distinctly: its title, its size and cover, as well as the effect it had on me. It introduced me to a way of approaching Christianity that I had never before encountered or even thought possible.

For, strange as it seems to me now, I was then largely unaware (as were most of the Westerners of my generation) of the significance of the ancient Christian teaching on the "divine indwelling," of God living at the very core of our being. I must have heard about this at some point, but I had very little understanding of its meaning and its importance, not only for Christians, but for all those drawn to explore the spiritual dimension of human life.

The book started a process in me that fundamentally changed and redirected my own search for God. It presented me with an amazing possibility: that Christ was, or could be, the way to the heart of my being where God lived. In other words, if I found Christ within—in my heart, in my own inner reality—I would have found the true meaning of my existence.

On the other hand, the book also made me more aware than I had ever been before that any true search for God must also be a search for true self-knowledge; unless I found my own true heart, my own reality, I could never find Christ in me or anywhere else and follow his way.

And so, when I finally accepted the fact that the little book was irretrievably lost, I promised myself that one day I would write it again. It is this promise that I set out to fulfill when I began writing this book. Very soon, however, I realized that I could not write of the original book again in any other way than my own. Not only because I could not remember enough of it, but, most of all, because I could not reflect on the journey of discovery on which it had started me without also reflecting on what I had learned since then: what Christ has come to mean to me.

QUESTION OF MEANING

As a small girl, like most children, I had a persistent habit of asking questions that tried the patience of many adults. "What is that?" I wanted to know, and "Why?" As I got to be a little older, I began to ask yet another question that was not always appreciated by my teachers, especially those who taught me religion. When presented with some "fact" (for they were presented to me as facts) that I was supposed to learn about God or Christ or the Church, I was very likely to raise my hand and ask, "But what does it *mean?*"

The answer I received most often was that this was a mystery revealed by God and that I must not question it or I might not go to heaven when I died. Instead of satisfying me, this answer only made me feel misunderstood and aggrieved. Why could the teacher not answer a simple question without getting mad? And how could God expect me to believe in something unless I knew what it meant?

What I did not understand then (and neither, it seems, did my teachers) was that when I asked, "What does it mean?" I was not asking for an explanation of a religious mystery. Still less was I expressing doubt about its truth, for that would not have occurred to me then. I simply wanted to understand its significance for me.

As I think of myself as I was then, it seems to me that in my own childish way, I was already searching for a way of making the religious truths I was taught my own: to mean something in my own life, my own reality. What difference did it make to me here, right now, I wanted to know, that God was a Trinity, that Christ was the Son of God, and that he died and rose from the dead? What difference did all these "facts" make not only after death, in some future life, but to my life here and now? How did it help me to understand myself and the amazing, sometimes terrifying world around me?

The question of meaning became even more urgent—and the religion I learned at school seemed even more irrelevant—when Germany invaded Poland in 1939 and World War II began. I was then eight years old. For the next seven years my family, as well as everyone we knew, lived through the horrors of Nazi occupation. Those were years of such ugliness and fear that the world of my catechism classes began to seem very remote, and reality ever more terrifying and incomprehensible.

And yet even during the darkest years there were times when beauty and joy would suddenly burst out of darkness unexpectedly, like lightning and, for a moment, the world was again full of wonder and meaning. It could be a moment when, on a bright summer morning, I awoke to the sound of a bird singing outside the window and the beauty of it pierced my heart.

It could be a moment on a late autumn afternoon when, as I was hurrying home just before curfew, I would look up and see the flaming glory of the setting sun and, for a split second, perhaps, be consoled and reassured. I have never forgotten these moments, for they gave me a glimpse of a reality that did not seem to have anything to do with the one in which we lived, and yet made our existence bearable.

※

A NEW BEGINNING

The war finally ended, although not in the way we had hoped. In September of 1946, my mother, brother and I escaped from communist Poland and eventually joined my father, who had spent the war years with the Polish Army in the West (first in France, and then in Britain, where he was now stationed). Upon our arrival in Britain, my parents decided to send me to a boarding school at Dumfries, Scotland, that was run by Catholic nuns. This way, they thought, I would learn English faster and make new friends. I loathed it at first, for I was angry, rebellious and scared. I had given up religion, I protested to my parents. What was I doing among all these nuns and their immature, silly girls?

But the nuns won me over in the end. In spite of myself, I was reassured by their kindness, their willingness to spend many hours helping me with my English and making me feel more at home. I was also moved by the way they prayed and sang in church. I began to appreciate the beauty and the sacred order of their religious services.

Sometimes, as I knelt with the other girls at evening prayers in the dimly lit church, the candles flickering before the holy images and shadows hiding in corners, the fear and confusion of the war years seemed to recede. I would find myself relaxing into silence and peace. "Christ is really here," I would think, and my heart would be filled with gratitude and love.

I spent only two years at Dumfries before my teachers decided I was ready for university. I left in tears, but promised myself and the nuns that I would come back to visit as often as I could. I kept my promise for as long as any of the nuns I knew were alive, but the little flame of religious faith that my stay with them had lit soon flickered and then died. For good, I thought at the time.

At the University, I encountered many other young people who claimed to have lost whatever faith they had had as children and who had concluded that religion had little to offer. I soon joined their ranks. Those were the days of philosophical and scientific positivism, when it was considered unscientific and even nonsensical to ask questions that could not be answered in terms of reason and proof that only science could provide. Any questions of a metaphysical or spiritual nature were therefore meaningless. God was not only dead, God had never existed.

It may be hard to imagine how a view of reality so devoid of any spiritual dimension could have attracted so many young people. But these were young men and women who had grown up in a world so dark, so absurd, that it was not difficult for them to conclude that life was, in fact, meaningless. It was perhaps easier to believe that there was no God than to believe in a God who allowed so much evil and suffering to exist in the world.

Those of us who could not accept such a bleak view of reality and continued to search for the "meaning of life"—and a surprising number of us still did—often sought it not in traditional religion but in our studies, in the beauty of nature, in literature, music and art. Surely, we thought, it was possible to find our own way to truth without having to resort to any doctrines or other trappings of religion.

It was not surprising, perhaps, that many of us became attracted to Eastern non-Christian religions, especially to Zen Buddhism, which seemed to be free of those trappings. A few of my friends even joined a Zen meditation group or took on another form of Eastern spiritual practice.

But for most of us, our search for meaning re-mained a largely theoretical one. We read, we talked and argued about spirituality and religion, just as we talked and argued about everything else. But once we left university and took up our lives as adults, most of us tended to turn our attention away from such meta-physical questions to more practical challenges and problems. These questions did not always disappear for good, however. For some of us at least, they were only filed away and would re-emerge in time.

"JUST SITTING"

My own passage to adulthood was made even more challenging than it could have been when yet another big change occurred in my life. As soon as I graduated from university, at the end of 1952, I left Britain to join the rest of my family in Canada, where they had emigrated three years earlier. Once again, I had to uproot myself and leave behind the country I had begun to think of as my own, and the friends I made there.

For the next 20 years, I was too preoccupied getting established, making new friends and, eventually, starting a family to have much time or energy for serious religious reflection. It was only when, in the early 1970s, I was faced with a painful and prolonged family crisis, that the question of meaning became urgent again. I began to be haunted by the need to find a way of understanding reality that would help me to come to terms with what I and my children were going through. But I was still unable or unwilling to search for it in any organized religion.

It was at that time that I became interested in Zen again and joined a Zen meditation group. What first drew me to take that step was the realization of how little I knew myself, how much I needed to learn to be more aware of what was going on in my own mind and heart. I had accumulated plenty of ideas and theories *about* myself, but I simply did not really know myself. Had I been more aware of my own true nature and needs, I realized, my life might be much simpler and less painful than it had become.

I also began to understand that no amount of thinking or self-analysis could help me to find out who I really was. I needed to find a way of becoming more attentive to myself, more in touch with what was happening in me and around me, at this very moment, right now. Zen seemed to offer me such a way.

The first thing I had to learn, as I began to "sit" at the Toronto Zen Centre, was that the "awareness" about which Zen Masters spoke was not some kind of esoteric or mystical experience of higher reality. It was rather a simple—but, for some of us, amazingly new—experience of being present, being attentive to all that was: what was going on in us and around us. Zen teaching was not about metaphysics or religion but about being aware, being awake to what was right now.

Practice of awareness consisted of "just sitting": sitting as still and as straight as we could and simply watching the flow of our breath as it went in and out of our lungs. We were to try to keep our minds from straying into thinking or interpreting our experience, or simply daydreaming. We were to be *just there*: sitting on our cushions and watching our breath.

I was surprised at how difficult this was for me, how unwilling my mind was to let go of its ideas and theories, how easily it wandered away from the simple reality of just being here, this very moment, right now. But I also discovered that through the practice of "just sitting," I was becoming more aware and present to reality, not only in my Zen practice but also in my everyday life. Eventually, I began to hope, I would come to realize the true meaning of who I was—not in terms of intellectual understanding or religious doctrine, but in terms of direct experience.

CHRIST KOAN

Yet although I embraced Zen practice and still felt no need for organized religion, I never stopped believing in God, for I do not think there was ever a time in my life when I did not believe in God. Neither did I ever reject or forget Christ, whom I did not know well but whose light-filled presence I believed I had encountered a few times in my life, and especially at Dumfries.

But who was Christ? I did not doubt that he was a great and holy man, a great spiritual teacher, perhaps the greatest who had ever lived. Yet that never seemed enough to explain my moments of encounter with him. On the other hand, the claim that he was God seemed too preposterous, too irrational to believe.

"Who is Christ?" became a kind of koan for me—one of those apparently unanswerable questions that Zen Masters set for their students to solve. The students nearly always begin—as I had done—by trying to figure out the answer by puzzling and agonizing over it with their thinking minds. They sit on their mats "thinking, thinking, thinking," as a Korean Master once said to me, even though they have been told countless times that thinking will not take them there, that only "not-thinking" will.

The purpose of assigning a koan is to make the students experience "not-thinking" for themselves. If they persevere in their practice, the masters say, they will eventually, often only after many years, come to a stone wall of not-knowing that they cannot break through with their heads. Beyond the wall lies a mystery, a level of reality not accessible to rational thought.

At that moment, if the students do not panic but remain silent and still at the wall, they may discover that although the answer to a koan cannot be found by thinking, it can be found. It can come to them in a moment of insight that arises from the deepest layer of their being, their true mind. And when it comes it dispels, even if only for a few seconds, all the unreality and confusion that usually fill the human mind. It is this moment of insight that, in the Buddhist tradition, is called enlightenment. We become simply aware of who we really are and realize that there is nothing else we need to be.

I did not stay in Zen practice long enough to experience a moment of such enlightenment or to find the answer to the koan of Christ, yet I stayed long enough to realize how I must look for it. I could not find it by thinking about it or by studying and reading books. The true answer would not be a concept or a definition *about* Christ, but Christ himself: realization of his presence with me and in me, at the core of my being.

It is at this point that I came across the little book *Christ Within* and discovered what was to become my own way of finding the meaning of Christ in my own life. I realized that as George Fox, the founder of the Society of Friends (Quakers), said, "there was something of God in every human soul." Finding this "something"—the divine life in me—was to be the goal of my inner path. But I did not yet know how to find that path, or even where to look for it.

✳

THE WAY BACK

I found the path, or at least the beginning of it, by literally walking into it when I visited Madonna House for the first time.[1] I had no idea at the time how decisive this apparently chance event would prove to be in my own life, the life of my family and only God knows who else's.

I had been aware of the existence of Madonna House for some years, as we had a family cottage at a lake nearby, but I was never interested enough to go there and find out for myself what this place really was. A rather eccentric Russian baroness, I had heard, had founded it 20 years earlier. I imagined a group of ladies in white dresses drinking tea on the lawn and talking about God, and thought to myself that I would rather give it a miss.

But on one very hot summer afternoon of 1964, my curiosity prevailed. On the way home from the village with my two children and the family dog, I drove in through a gate that had a sign proclaiming "Pax et Caritas" above it. There were no ladies in white dresses that I could see, just a few young people wearing jeans working in the garden. I noticed a house with a blue door and, down by the river, a group of people having tea. My son and the dog made a dash for the river and I followed, rather hesitantly, with my ten-month-old daughter on my arm. We were promptly invited to join the party.

It is hard to describe the impact the encounter with Madonna House and with its foundress had on me. In Catherine Doherty I met a woman who was very human and real but also a wise teacher and a "reader of hearts." I saw a community that seemed to live a very down-to-earth kind of life, a life of everyday acceptance and love that I had never witnessed before. It was, as Catherine Doherty often said, a way of "living the Gospel without compromise": a group of men and women who seemed committed to spending their lives trying to love.

Of course, I did not learn it all on that first day. There were many times when I felt disappointed (for they were not always very holy, I complained; they did not always show the kind of love they preached). Many times I swore that I would never return. But, in the end, I always did. For, as I learned during the many years of my friendship with Madonna House, no human being can ever be "holy" every day; no one can love another perfectly.

Although I never joined Madonna House (I could not even if I wanted to, as all the members of the community are single), I became and have remained a close friend of the community, or so I hope. I do not always agree with all their views, I certainly do not represent them when I write, but I admire and love them. I have learned from them more than I can say. Above all else, I learned that to love others we must be willing to fail at loving again and again and yet not become discouraged. We must be willing to forgive others for failing, but, even more significantly, to forgive ourselves, again and again. It was in living this life of "ceaseless forgiveness"—or trying to live it—that Madonna House made love very real. They made Christ very real. They made the Gospel very real.

✳

ORTHODOX WAY

It was also at Madonna House that I first encountered the tradition of Eastern (Orthodox) Christianity and, through it, the teaching of the early Christian teachers and saints. I realized that the insight I had found in the book *Christ Within*—that God in Christ was present at the core of our own being—was not a side issue to Christianity but its central, fundamental teaching.

I learned this not only at Madonna House, where the Russian Orthodox roots of the foundress were treasured and highly visible in the daily life of the community, but also from my own reading and from some Orthodox friends and teachers I met. The two who had the greatest impact on me were Metropolitan Anthony Bloom, whom I met in London and visited several times, and Mother Maria Gysi, an Orthodox nun, foundress of the Monastery of the Assumption in the North of England.

I never met Mother Maria while she was alive (she died at her monastery in 1977), yet I believe I got to know her well. I read and reread her writings, visited the monastery several times and learned all I could from Mother Thekla, her first disciple and her successor as abbess. I learned to know and love Mother Maria as one is sometimes fortunate to get to know and love a saint. To paraphrase her own words describing the Communion of Saints, "she walked into my life one day and has never left."

Although I did not become Orthodox, but returned to the Catholicism into which I was born, what I learned—and continue to learn—from the Orthodox tradition about the essential nature of Christian life has never left me. This teaching made it possible for me to begin to overcome the attitude of mistrust and even hostility to organized religion that I had carried for so long. I started to understand the significance of the Church as the visible sign and means of Christ's presence in our human reality. Orthodox liturgy, music and sacred art—the icon—helped me to realize the importance of the concrete, physical expression of faith.

The Orthodox insistence on the inability of the human mind to understand the mysteries of faith showed me that my mistrust of religious and dogmatic authoritarianism was not totally mistaken; that it was supported by the early Christian tradition of faith. Faith is a grace; it can never be fully grasped with our rational mind or defined in words. It can only be accepted and embraced with our own hearts. It can never be imposed on others.

The attitude of respect for the inner freedom of each human being, which seemed to be fundamental to the teaching and lives of the early Orthodox saints, encouraged me to respect my own inner freedom: to try to listen ever more carefully to my own inner voice and to seek the way to truth that my heart could fully and unreservedly embrace. It also taught me that such freedom and respect for oneself was fundamental to the Christian vocation of love. We could not love and respect others if we did not love and respect ourselves.

Yet, there remained many unresolved issues that kept me from returning to the practice of Christianity for the next few years. I continued to see the Church as I remembered it from my childhood: arbitrary, with authoritarian structure and a priesthood that I had resented and rebelled against. My mind still refused to accept any teaching that I was told I "had" to believe.

I still did not like the kind of piety and devotion I encountered in Catholic churches that seemed to me naive, sentimental and mind-befuddling. I still resented having rules of moral behaviour that I did not always agree with imposed on me. I was afraid, or rather I was sure, that it would be an impossible struggle for my mind to accept the limits to its freedom that I thought becoming a practising Catholic again would involve.

※

NOT AN OBSTACLE

My doubts and hesitations seemed confirmed when one of my friends from the Zen Centre came to see me one day. He was concerned about my decision to return to Christianity. "Don't you think," he asked, "that committing yourself to any religion might prove to be an obstacle on your way? That you might get stuck on Christian teaching and Christian beliefs and never find your own true path?"

I was quite disturbed by this question and did not know how to answer it, for it seemed to express the fundamental doubt that lay under all the other doubts I was struggling with at the time. If I were to accept unconditionally everything that Christian tradition taught, would I have to surrender my right to follow my own inner voice? Would I be able to find my own way to God?

Later on, when I learned more about Christianity, I began to see that the notion of religion being an "obstacle" to truth was not as outrageous as I had imagined. It is true that we may get so preoccupied with our own beliefs and ideas about Christ, so concerned with our own orthodoxy, that we are unable to see the immense mystery of God's presence and love that Christ came to share with us.

Or we may get so caught up in our own good deeds, our devotions, our spiritual progress, the emotions we experience in our prayers and meditations, that we forget that the real goal of the Christian path is not our own righteousness or spiritual wisdom, but only God. In other words, it is not Christianity I might become "stuck" on, but myself.

But I did not understand this at the time. And so my friend's warning increased my uncertainty and I began to doubt the reality of my own conversion. I analyzed and questioned the motives that had led me to it. Was my conversion a result of a real change of heart on my part, a true grace, or was it a product of my own need? Was I seeking God or an escape from the aloneness that has plagued me for most of my life? Was I looking for a sense of belonging, of being accepted, of having a spiritual home at last?

If these were real reasons for my return to Christianity, I began to suspect that I had chosen the wrong way to achieve them. I seemed to be as alone as I was before. If I no longer felt at home with friends whose lives and preoccupations did not seem to leave any space for God, neither did I feel at home with many of my Christian friends. I had not found the certainty and peace that their faith seemed to give them. I did not feel sure I had made the right choice; I was not free of doubt.

※

THE JESUS PRAYER

I do not know where all these struggles and doubts might have led me, whether I would have persevered or turned away, had I not encountered the practice of the Jesus Prayer at the very beginning of my Christian path. The best-known and beloved prayer of the Orthodox Church, it has been practised in the Christian East for centuries, and is now becoming familiar to many in the West. (In fact, I was introduced to the prayer by a Roman Catholic priest.)

The Jesus Prayer is a very simple prayer that consists of constant, silent repetition of these words: *Lord Jesus Christ, Son of God, have mercy on me, a sinner!* Or, in its shorter form, *Lord Jesus Christ, have mercy on me!* It is not important which form we adopt, as long as the name of Jesus is invoked. This is why the prayer has been called a "confession of faith" in Christ. When we call upon the name of Jesus, when we place ourselves in his presence and ask for his mercy, we recognize him for who he is: the Son of God, God dwelling in our own human flesh. We call upon the name of Jesus because it is a "name above all other names" (Philippians 2:9). It is the highest expression of the ineffable name of God of which human beings are capable.

It is important, the writers on the prayer empha-size, to say the words as attentively as we can, without trying to evoke any emotions or spiritual experiences. We are not to try to imagine or feel Christ's presence with us in any tangible way. We need only to remind ourselves that, whether we know it or not, he is al-ways there: always present and attentive to us, aware of our every thought and of every movement of our heart.

We can pray the Jesus Prayer while walking or sitting or even lying down. The position does not matter as long as it allows us to focus our attention on the prayer. The Jesus Prayer is a way of attention, of waking up and not of relaxing and going to sleep. In other words, it is a way of awareness. We practise it in order to open ourselves to Christ's presence, wherever and however he reveals himself to us.[2] And so, if our mind wanders off the words—which happens, as we soon find out, more often than not—we simply return to them without any fuss and continue saying them quietly, peacefully, with as much attention as we can. We pray the prayer as often as we remember to do so, but we also try, especially at the beginning, to set aside some time every day to practise it.

While it is important to become disciplined in our practice, we must not become obsessive about how and how often we pray it. As Father Lev Gillet has suggested, we need to learn to respect our own inner needs and find our own way of praying the Jesus Prayer. We allow ourselves to fall silent—to let the words go—whenever we feel drawn to it. The Jesus Prayer is intended to lead us into silence: to remind us of silence, sustain us in silence and not prevent us from reaching it. The prayer will not leave us if we cease to pray the words for a moment. It goes on within us, on its own, and will soon begin to sound in us again.[3]

ENTERING THE INNER ROOM

The Jesus Prayer has often been called "the prayer of the heart." Its early teachers instructed their disciples to pray it while focusing their inner attention on their hearts, the centre of their being—and addressing the prayer to Christ living there. If they prayed that way, they might eventually find and enter the "inner room" about which Christ spoke (Matthew 6:6) and experience the reality of Christ's presence within them.

Yet we need not rush to follow these instructions too closely. As contemporary teachers of the prayer often point out, these early practitioners were nearly always monks or hermits. The prayer was undertaken and practised under the direction and daily supervision of the elders, the most experienced monks. They may have been able to push their disciples to physical and spiritual lengths that would be very difficult and even dangerous for us to imitate.

We also need to keep in mind that we approach this prayer from the perspective of a different age, a different way of life and, if we are not Orthodox, another Christian tradition from that of those early monks. We should not presume that we are able to take on the practice of the Jesus Prayer in the same way as those who had known it all their lives and had made it their life's work.

Of course, if we feel drawn to it, we need not hesitate to begin to pray it, or feel we must settle for something less than the ancient monks aspired to. But we must practise it more simply, more humbly, perhaps, and not worry too much if we are unable to pray it as well as we wish, or if we cannot manage to pray it all the time. All we need to do is to accept our own limitations and the limitations our life imposes on us, and remind ourselves that, as its early teachers used to say, the Jesus Prayer is not a prayer of those who are perfect but a prayer of sinners.

If we persevere—whether we practise it magnificently, with all our energy and concentration, or very poorly, hesitatingly, unsure of what we are doing—we will eventually realize that we have learned to pray the prayer much of the time. The prayer continues in us by itself, in the same way as our breathing continues by itself, whether we are aware of it or not. We may forget the prayer for a while, but it does not forget us; we shall soon find ourselves praying it again during our everyday activities and wake up at night saying it.

Sometimes, especially at the beginning, we may get tired of the practice. There have been many times in my life when I have felt utterly discouraged and bored, when the words of the prayer seemed to hammer at my mind like a tune I could not stop humming. At such times, I felt chained to the prayer, smothered by its monotony, unable to think. I was not praying, I suspected, but trying to escape the emptiness I felt inside me by drowning it with the mindless repetition of a few words.

And yet, whenever these times passed—and they always did, in the end—I could not help but realize how fruitful they had been. Although the practice did not seem to lead me into any greater awareness of Christ's presence as quickly as I had hoped, it led me into a greater awareness of what was happening in my own heart.

✳

PLACE OF REALITY

The heart, as it was understood in early Christian teaching, does not refer to our physical heart or the centre of our emotional life. Rather, it is the heart of our being, the centre of our whole human reality: body, soul and spirit. It is an opening—a door—through which our finite human reality meets the ultimate reality of God; it is our own "I," our "true self," that God breathed into us at the moment of creation.

Some religious or other traditions see the "true self" or the "true heart" as a mysterious, perfect self that we must struggle to achieve, or a higher state of consciousness we must reach. In the Christian tradition, however, our true heart is our own everyday, ordinary heart, the centre of our being. It is capable of great holiness and love, but also of corruption and sin. It is often frightened, rebellious and unreal, ignorant of its own true reality. It is this human heart that we must find and make real again, by opening it to God.

Sometimes when we talk of being real, we mean being realistic, seeing the world and ourselves in a down-to-earth, common-sense way. We assume that the word *reality* refers mainly to our earthly reality: our everyday life in the world. Some people may go even further, insisting that there is no other, "higher" level of reality. For them, belief in such a thing is an attempt to escape from the real world into a non-existent world of fantasy and myth.

But from a religious perspective, spiritual reality is not a fantasy or an illusion; it is as real as, or even more real than, the reality we can touch, hear and see, imagine or deduce with our rational minds. Neither is it understood as something totally beyond or outside of our earthly reality. It is, rather, the deepest level—the heart—of our ordinary reality. It is our ordinary reality, grounded in and pervaded by the reality of God: the ultimate cause and final purpose of all existence. We cannot remain truly real if we forget or deny that reality.

Existence that is perceived as having no ultimate cause and no final purpose is not real; it is absurd and thus cannot exist. The notion of a causeless universe—which seems to mean a universe that comes forth through "chance" and not through a creative act of God—may be posited by scientists as a working hypothesis, but cannot be lived by—cannot be life-giving—for it denies the deepest truth of our own hearts.

On the other hand, it is also misleading to suppose, as some spiritual traditions appear to do, that *only* this higher spiritual reality is truly real: that the ordinary, everyday world in which we live, the ordinary self that we are, is an illusion into which humanity has fallen (usually in some distant, long-forgotten past) and from which it must be liberated. Such liberation, it is believed, is the aim of all true religion.

Christian tradition does not understand spiritual reality in that way. Christian beliefs do not contradict or deny the significance of our earthly reality, but fulfill it. They are mysteries: signs of another level of being made manifest in our midst. In Christ, God has become implanted within us—at the heart of ourselves. From there, God pervades our whole reality, our soul, body, mind, imagination and will: every level of our existence. We cannot find God, we cannot find Christ, unless we are willing to be real.

※

TRUE PRAYER

This point is especially important to remember when we begin to pray. How can we find Christ in our hearts, how can we open ourselves to his presence, unless we are willing to be real? What good will it do to present Christ with some idealized, pious view of ourselves? What good will it do if we try to hide our faults from him, assume virtues we do not possess, pretend to feel emotions we do not feel, or pray in a way that means nothing to us? How can we ever find Christ, who is Truth, in that kind of pretend reality?

This is why we must learn to pray in the way that is most real to us, that is a true expression of our own longing for God: of the way we are best able to experience his presence but also of our difficulties and struggles, our failures and sins. It is this kind of real prayer that may rightly be called the prayer of the heart. For some of us, the Jesus Prayer can best lead to the heart of ourselves, the way of learning to be real in God's presence. But it is not and never has been the only way, or even the best way, for everyone.

We need to be careful not to presume or imagine that, because we find God and experience his presence most often through this or that way of prayer, we can consider ourselves to have a better, a more direct line to God. I once had a clear and embarrassing lesson on this point from an elderly lady who had spent most of her life on a farm near the village where I now live. One day, as I was having a cup of tea with her, I asked what she did in the evenings. Did she watch television or read books?

"Oh no," she replied, "I don't have time for reading books. I have too many prayers to read!"

"You read all your prayers?" I asked, aghast. "Don't you ever talk to God in your own words? Or just be silent with God?" (In my defence, I can only say that I was much younger then and I hope would not think of asking such a question now.)

She looked at me, perplexed. "But I always read my prayers *to him*," she said, "for he is always there!" And then she smiled and added, "I am not as educated and clever as you are, you see. I don't know as many words as you do."

This embarrassing encounter taught me a lesson I never forgot. It taught me that it would be a misunderstanding of Christian teaching to conclude that we can find Christ in our hearts only through introspection or some other extraordinary way of meditation or prayer. Christ may be found in the ordinary reality of our lives, in our ordinary religious practice or in the world around us.

For Christ cannot be contained in any one human heart, in any one person's reality. He cannot be imprisoned somewhere inside us, as if in a tabernacle or a box. Christ is in us, but he is also among us. He is present and can be found in every human heart.

He is the bond of presence and love that holds us all together: the Church on earth but also in heaven.

✳

CHRIST AMONG US

Christ is among us. He has made love the greatest and the essential commandment, and we had better not forget it. For Christ made it absolutely clear that if we want to be his disciples, if we want to enter the kingdom of heaven, we must learn how to love one another. Even the smallest act of love for another, given or refused—a visit, a piece of bread, a cup of water—will be counted.

When we die, Christ told us, we shall not be asked what exactly we thought or imagined or felt about him, or how often we went to church, or whether we have had any profound spiritual experiences. We shall be asked only whether we recognized him and loved him in each other.

This may be a hard and frightening question for us to answer, for we often seem to find it difficult to accept that Christ lives in everyone else's heart, everyone else's reality, as well as in our own. He does not live in us because we are special, more prayerful, more faithful or more intelligent and educated than others, or even, as we may secretly imagine, because he loves us more!

It may seem absurd and offensive to even suggest such a point of view, but if we look into ourselves a little more deeply, we may be amazed how many such absurd presumptions lurk in some dark corner of our soul. And if they do, we must face them and give them up as soon as we can. As Christ never tired of teaching his disciples, unless we find him and love him in each other, we cannot find him and love him at all.

Having taken on our human nature, Christ has entered the heart of every human being and identified himself with each person so totally that everything we do or fail to do for another, we do or fail to do for him. To love others is to recognize Christ's presence in them as we do in ourselves. For Christ really is in us all.

When St. Francis kissed the leper he met on the road because he saw Christ in him, Francis was not imagining it or making an act of faith. He saw Christ dwelling at the core of his suffering brother's reality. He saw that Christ and the leper were one. This is as true now as it was then, although few have the eyes to see it. Mother Teresa was one of those, and so was Catherine Doherty. In their lives and in all they said or wrote, they endlessly reminded us of this fundamental truth of Christ's teaching. To love and serve another is to love and serve Christ. Perhaps there is no other way of seeing things if you are a saint.

Yet even that great truth does not exhaust the mystery of who Christ is. Christ is within us and among us, he is present and must be loved in us all, but he is also beyond us: he is a mystery infinitely greater than what our minds can grasp or our human hearts can contain. The whole universe cannot contain Christ. He is the divine *Logos*: the Word of God, the full expression of the Wisdom of God, the pattern on whom all reality is based and whom it reflects, the goal to whom it moves and in whom it will be fulfilled.

✳

CHRIST BEYOND US

Yet to say that Christ is a mystery beyond ourselves is not to place him outside of our own reality. He is not a supernatural or magical manifestation or force from heaven, or a visitor from outer space coming to save us from the miserable world we have been stranded in.

From a religious perspective, *mystery* does not mean a puzzle, an unsolved problem that mystifies us and demands a solution. *Mystery* means a level of reality that we cannot reach with our rational minds, solve or explain in words, but that we can encounter and experience if we only know how to look: open-eyed, the way small children look at the world.

We can see this in the face of a newborn baby—what can be more mysterious and at the same time more real? We can see it in a work of great literature or art. We can see it in the beauty and splendour of a sunset, hear it in the vast silence of the night sky or in the roar of a storm at sea. Nature, Archbishop Joseph Raya used to say, is the "fifth Gospel."[4]

I first learned about the power and beauty of nature from my grandmother when I was a child in Poland. She lived alone in the mountains in a house built by local craftsmen on the edge of a torrent. The noise of its rushing waters was the background of every moment of our holidays and the first sound of eternity I learned to hear. My grandmother was brilliant and wise; she loved literature and art and was fascinated by science. Above all else, she loved the beauty of the mountains among which she lived and among which she eventually died.

During one of our holidays with her, when I was only five or six, I was awakened one night by my grandmother leaning over my bed. There was a noise of a great storm outside. Grandmother picked me up and carried me out onto the big verandah at the front of the house. "Look!" she said, turning my face towards the mountains. "Look, this is too beautiful to sleep through!" I saw black sky, torn apart every few seconds by lightning, mountains emerging out of darkness, immense, powerful and so real.

I looked up at my grandmother's face and, in a flash of light, saw it flooded with wonder and joy. I did not realize then, of course, that what I saw and heard that night was God. My grandmother was the first to teach me the immense mystery and glory and sometimes terror of God at the heart of creation.

Most of us may have had similar experiences, although we may not be able to express them in words or art. We may not always understand precisely what we are seeing or hearing; we do not always know its name. But it is always the same mystery, the mystery and the glory of the whole of reality. It is the presence of God filling the universe.[5] For us who are Christians, it is Christ: the mystery of the Infinite taking flesh in the finite; the Invisible shining through the visible; Christ, the ultimate meaning of all.

Our search for Christ within is not a quest for some mystical experience or a profound insight into the mystery of Christ's being or nature. It is not an attempt to contain him within our small, finite self. We find Christ within whenever and wherever our hearts can recognize him and begin to "burn within us," as the hearts of the disciples burned when he walked with them on the way to Emmaus before they even knew who he really was (Luke 24:32).

MYSTERY-EVENT

B ecause Christ is the infinite Word of God, time and space and any other finite dimension have no power over him. In the Incarnation, the infinite enters the finite, heaven joins itself to earth, eternity makes itself present in time. This means that every event of the Incarnation—every moment of Christ's life on earth—is both a historical event that happened in the past, in the concrete everyday human reality, and also a mystery, a happening, in the infinite and unknowable *now* of God. It is not either one or the other; it is both.

We see this truth most clearly expressed in the liturgical life of the Church, although we do not always realize or remember it. I had not understood its significance until the first time I attended the Orthodox Liturgies of Holy Week in a small parish in Toronto.

I went with some misgivings: it was a very poor parish, the choir was not very good, the congregation not very interesting or sophisticated. Would I be able to stand all those hours in church? Would it be too tiring, too boring, too long? But I did go. I stood hour after hour, every day, every night, and all night of Holy Saturday. I bowed and crossed myself countless times. I sang as best I could. I was there.

I was at the Last Supper. I followed Christ to the Garden. I stood with the other women by the cross. I wept and wailed with them when we were burying him. I ran with them to the tomb. I saw it empty! I realized with every fibre of my being that the Paschal Mystery was not the past, but was the present reality in which I lived every moment of my life. As Mother Maria would have put it, I experienced a "mystery-event."

> The life of Christ, lived on earth, is real and divine. Its historic reality, its uniqueness, the "once for all" of His life is not bound to the past. His life is open, in its total reality: for us to step into it. And, then, we discover that, although unaware, we have been surrounded all the time by His life, as by the vast sea.... The event bears the Mystery and the Mystery bears the event. For us, it is no repeated, remembered, reenacted, or symbolic event. It is the event.[6]

What a rich, life-giving insight that is! The life of Christ is not history to us, it is our present. It is right here with us and in us and among us. The liturgy and the sacraments are the door to the life of Christ—a wide and open door. We are invited to walk through this door, to live this life, every time we participate in the sacramental and liturgical life of the Church. These are, or can be, moments out of time for us, when we "fold the wings of our intellect," as Catherine Doherty used to say, and enter the mystery of

Christ's presence that our minds cannot comprehend by themselves, but our hearts can embrace and live.

It is true that not all of us can experience the liturgy in that deep and moving way. I myself did not experience it as deeply and vividly ever again. But I have never doubted that my Easter experience was real, that Christ had been there and that I had been there; that I had accompanied him in the moment of his greatest need.

※

HE WILL "AROSE" ON SUNDAY!

I was reminded of this experience on Good Friday three or four years ago. My little grandson John was sitting on the floor putting on his shoes to go outside. As he struggled with his shoelaces, he looked up at the icon of the cross that my daughter had placed, with the vigil light burning before it, on a little desk by the door. John nodded towards the icon and said, "That is Jesus. He is dead, you know!" And then, perhaps concerned that his announcement might have distressed me, he added, "But it is okay, because he is God and will 'arose' on Sunday!" Having said all that needed to be said, he ran outside, banging the door.

My grandson clearly had no trouble accepting the double-dimensional nature of the mystery-event that we were celebrating. Our adult thinking minds, fixed in their limited, time-bound perception of reality, find this concept much more difficult to grasp. Some may never be able to grasp it or believe it at all.

Because our reason cannot hold onto the mystery—cannot possess it or prove it—our rational mind seems compelled to question our experience of this mystery, to doubt it, to put it aside and ignore it. Or we might try to intellectualize it: to make it sound so rational, explaining it in such belaboured ways, that it may appear not more rational but less so, to others and even to ourselves.

This is why I believe it is important to participate regularly in the liturgical and sacramental life of the Church, to celebrate its feasts and celebrations, to keep up its ancient traditions, postures of prayer and gestures of reverence. In other words, we must leave our rational, questioning minds behind for a time and approach the mystery we are celebrating simply, as my grandson approached it, by embracing it and participating in it.

And yet we must not become so involved in the beauty and power of these liturgical events, so full of pious emotions, that we imagine we have understood and assimilated their meaning more fully than others who do not share our enthusiasm or who cannot agree with us about what the sacraments mean and how they act.

We need to remind ourselves that Christ is always present and available to us. That is the fundamental mystery of our faith, the only real basis on which we can build our lives as Christians. The sacraments are doors to the mystery; they are not the mystery itself.

Christ is not bound by any event, however sacred it may be; he can make himself present to us and in us and among us wherever and however he wants. We can experience his presence in simple, individual prayer, in meditation, in books. He can come to us in our studies, in the flow of ideas in our minds. We can encounter him in happiness and sorrow, in beauty, in a moment of joy or of human love. He is the same Christ, the One mystery at the heart of creation, for there is no other.

✳

TIMELESS GOSPEL

O ur faith in the boundless and timeless nature of Christ's presence helps us to understand more clearly the significance of the Gospels in Christian tradition. Christians have not spent so much care and effort through the centuries safeguarding and passing on the Gospels only because they describe events that have had a profound influence on the last two thousand years of human history. Christians have not defended the Gospels, sometimes with their lives, only because they contain deep moral truths fundamental to our sanctity and happiness.

Christians have clung to the Gospels, studied them, resisted all attempts at reducing them to merely historical documents of uncertain origins, because they realized that the events in the life of Christ—everything that happened to him, all his miracles and all his words—are timeless: they are always present. They are, in a way we cannot understand but can experience, always happening in our midst.

Through the Gospels, as through the sacraments, we can enter the timeless, boundless life of the Son of God present with us. We can enter it, immerse ourselves in it and live it out in our lives. Each page of the Gospels is not just a page from a book—mere words on paper. Each page is a crossing point where time and eternity, the finite and the infinite, the human and the divine meet.

When we say that the Gospels are "inspired"—the work of the Holy Spirit—we do not mean that every single detail in them has been written directly by God. We mean that the Gospels—all the events that they describe, all the miracles of Christ and all his teachings—are vessels of the Spirit, filled with the truth of Christ's life and making it present to us. In this way they share the nature of the sacraments: the Gospels are sacramental.

That is why we stand up when the book of the Gospels is carried in and placed on the altar; we bow down before it and kiss it with reverence. If we have a copy of the Gospels in our homes, we take care of it; we don't just leave it lying around. And each time we read or hear the Gospel, we proclaim and witness to the mystery of Christ "who was at the beginning, is now, and forever shall be." We do not just remember or commemorate the mystery, we participate in it.

There is, of course, little use in venerating the Gospels if we never read them. This may seem obvious, and yet it must be stated. It is surprising how few of us read the Gospels: not just in church, but as part of our regular practice.

The Catholic Church has to carry a substantial part of the blame for this sad state of affairs. For centuries, it discouraged and even at times forbade its laity to study the scriptures on their own. Even to possess a copy of the Bible could have led to a charge of heresy.

This is one of the dark parts of Catholic history. Although it is, thankfully, now past, we have never quite recovered from it. We need to recover from it, however, and make reading the Gospels a regular part of our everyday life. If we do not, we deprive ourselves of a powerful means of entering the timeless mystery of Christ's presence and participating in his life.

※

ICONS OF CHRIST

In the Eastern Christian tradition, this sacramental nature of the Gospels is shared to some degree by the icon, the traditional art of the Orthodox Church. In recent years, many Western Christians have also been drawn to the icon, although they may know little of its history or of the tradition that created it. They may not realize that the icon, according to Orthodox teaching, is not a form of religious art as we understand it in the West. It is not simply a product of an artist's imagination of various events in the life of Christ, or an expression of the artist's feelings towards Christ or towards his Mother or the saints. The Orthodox believe that the icon, like the Gospels, makes the event it depicts present; it is a mystery-event.

A "true icon"—that is, an icon that is true to the mind of the Orthodox Church—is the work of someone firmly grounded in the faith of the tradition, who prepares for it by prayer and fasting and paints it (or "writes" it, as the Orthodox say) with reverence and a sense of a mystery of God taking flesh through the work of his or her heart and hands. When completed, the icon is consecrated and anointed in church. It is thus seen as the work both of human hands and of God; it is a work of grace.

When we stand and pray before an icon, we enter the event it represents. We participate in it; we are there. We are there at the moment when the angel announces the Incarnation; we are present at the Nativity; we follow Christ into the wilderness; we see him crucified and carry him to the tomb. We meet him risen in the garden; we touch his wounds.

Not all Christians can view the icon in this way. Not all find it useful or even right to revere the icon or any other religious representation of the divine as sacramental. For some, such a practice seems to contradict the biblical tradition that rejects and even forbids any material representations of God. Even those who do accept images or "holy pictures" in their worship and prayer life may find the belief in their sacramental nature difficult to understand or to accept. How can wood and paint make God present? How can they be viewed as a means of grace?

And yet, we may remind ourselves, the whole sacramental life of the Church is based on the belief that because the spirit of God dwells in and penetrates all of creation, the material elements of the world—the water of baptism, the bread and wine of the Eucharist, the holy oils of anointing—have the power to carry within themselves the immaterial. The finite can be a vessel of the infinite.

＊

PERFECT EXPRESSION

For both Catholic and Orthodox Christians, the clearest and highest expression of the mystery of Christ living out his life and death in us—in our own human reality—is found in the person of Mary, the Mother of Christ. Every event of Christ's life was also an event of Mary's life, a fact of her everyday reality as well as of her innermost heart.

At the moment of Christ's conception, the Spirit enters her, and the angel, as the Orthodox Church sings, "is rapt in amazement" at the mystery of God taking flesh in the womb of a woman. She gives birth to Christ in Bethlehem. She carries him into the Temple and presents him to God. She becomes an exile in Egypt with him; she nurses and makes a home for him in Nazareth.

Mary lives his "secret life" with her son. She goes with him to Jerusalem and searches the streets for him when he seems to be lost. She finds him in the Temple—the New Covenant present at the centre of the Old. She lets him endlessly break her heart, leave her, even apparently rebuff her at times. And yet, she is always there for him; she runs to him in his need; she keeps him in her heart. She ponders on all that is happening to him.

Mary stands at the cross and suffers the dreadful pain and humiliation with him; she is the Mother of Compassion, co-sufferer of Christ's pain. She receives his body into her arms; she buries him; she rejoices at his resurrection and his ascension into glory. She is there when the Spirit descends on the Apostles and the Church is born.

And, according to an early tradition, after Christ's death, Mary lives for many years in the home of St. John as the Mother and support of the Church. On her death and assumption (or *dormition*, as the Orthodox prefer to call it), Mary becomes the icon or the sign of the final resurrection promised to all those who live and die with Christ. She is the first of us all to receive the crown of eternal, resurrected life. Connected as closely as it is possible to be to God, she remains forever herself: Mary, the Mother of us all.

Sometimes both Orthodox and Catholic Christians are accused of going beyond what is proper and even rational in their devotion to Mary, of seeming to make her into an idol, nearly an equal partner in Christ's work of salvation, which gives her an importance that can be given only to Christ. This is a very real danger. Nevertheless, many believe, the risk is worth taking, for to deny to honour her or to reject her significance and place in the mystery of our salvation goes against both the tradition and the inner instinct of millions of Christian lives.

When we rejoice in Mary, we rejoice in the mystery of Christ. She is the Theotokos, the Bearer, the

Mother of God. We praise her in our prayers and hymns, in her many feasts, in countless images and statues and shrines. We heap titles upon her. She is the Virgin, the Queen of Heaven, the Mother of Mercy, the Mother of Hope, the Refuge of all Christians. But we must not forget that it is Christ in her that we celebrate.

This is why, in the Orthodox tradition, there are very few icons that show Mary alone. Even in those few (as in the icons of the Annunciation or the Visitation), Christ is already present in her; he has taken flesh in her flesh. In all her icons, she always points to him. In the Catholic tradition, although she is a subject of countless holy pictures and statues and an object of ardent and, at times, overly sentimental devotion, Mary is always intended to be understood in the context of the mystery of Christ. Thus the most popular Catholic devotion, the Rosary, is meant to be a way of remembering and pondering on the events of the life she has shared with her son.

We love and venerate Mary because we see in her not only the perfect icon of the life of her son, but also the perfect icon of our own human life: the perfect expression of who we are to become. Mary exemplifies for us the final destiny of each one of us: to know Christ, to love him, to unite ourselves with him as fully as we can, and thus to live his life and death in our own human reality (Galatians 2:20).

When we live in communion with Christ and share his life, everything he did, said and experienced becomes an event that takes place not only in eternity but also here on earth. In our own life we make the mysteries of his life present again; we become true "gospels" and icons of Christ. We "write" the sacred image in our own flesh and blood.

※

WISDOM OF THE BODY

As I get older, I become ever more aware of the essential holiness of our whole human reality and of the danger of neglecting or excluding any one aspect of it from our spiritual life. It is fairly easy for us to recognize the danger of the tendency, so prevalent today, to minimize or even to deny the importance of spiritual reality and thus to reduce human nature to merely body and brain.

But we do not always see that it is just as dangerous for us to cut ourselves off from our material reality, from our own body and flesh, the dust out of which we were made. Perhaps when we come to the end of our lives we, like St. Francis, may have to ask our body's forgiveness for the way we have treated it during our time on earth. We may have to admit how much poorer our life has been due to our cutting ourselves off from the timeless wisdom of the body.

The body is not just something our souls have to bear with until they are free to discard it at the end of our earthly lives; it is an inseparable aspect of our whole human self. It is not an envelope of flesh and skin that protects us and separates our inner reality from the rest of the universe; it is our connecting link with the universe, our organ of communication with the whole of reality. Without the body we could not utter a word; we could not think or learn. Without the body we would not be real human beings; we would be only ghosts.

The body has been with us from the beginning of our life on earth and remembers everything we have ever experienced or thought. It remembers our every sorrow and our every joy. The body holds the record—the code—of our earthly life. And not only of our own short life. The body holds and remembers in its every cell and every gene all that has happened in our own bodies, in the bodies of our direct ancestors, and in the universal movement of life.

I was given an inkling of this timeless wisdom of the body in an experience I had many years ago during a Buddhist meditation retreat. The retreat involved many hours of sitting meditation, no talking, little sleep and even less food. One morning we were wakened, as usual, before dawn and sent out of doors to do our walking meditation on the grounds of the centre and in the fields just beyond. I walked slowly, as I was taught, trying to be aware of every step, every movement I made. I was highly conscious of the ground under my feet, of the trees surrounding the fields, of the birds just beginning to wake.

In a little while, the eastern sky became a glory of colour and light as the sun rose over the fields. I looked at it for a moment, and then my body spontaneously moved into a dance. I bowed and raised my arms, I swayed, I began to chant. It was a moment of great beauty and grace that taught me a lesson that, although I have never experienced it as powerfully since, I shall never forget. The body, I realized, was an indispensable aspect of my own reality and a means of grace.

The body is holy and wise; it knows the truth about ourselves that can take our minds the rest of our lives to learn. No discipline, no therapy, no prayer or any other spiritual practice is truly real—truly our own—unless our body is involved in it. We cannot find the meaning of our life, we cannot find our true heart, we cannot find Christ, unless we also find him in our bodily reality: in our "outer man," as St. Paul called it (2 Corinthians 4:16). If we exclude our body from our spiritual life or from the way we pray, we make that life poorer and less real.[7]

※

THE WORD MADE FLESH

Praying the Jesus Prayer has taught me to become more aware of this important, all-inclusive aspect of spiritual life. I understood that I could not truly attend to the spiritual dimension of the Jesus Prayer unless I also attended to the way my body and mind participated in it. I needed to pay attention not only to the meaning of the words I was saying, but also to how they flowed in and out of my body with each breath, and how they seemed to merge with the beating of my heart.

This is true of every other way of praying as well. Each time we enter the presence of God—no matter which words we use or whether we remain silent—we begin to realize that in order to pray well, we must pray from the whole of our human reality, both physical and spiritual. When we stand before the infinite mystery of God, we do not leave our finite nature behind. We are, and must remain, stretched out between the earthly reality of our everyday life and the mystery that lies beyond.

The mystery is always there, always calling to us and yet always beyond our reach. This truth is often very painful for us to experience. We may feel trapped in our human nature, weighed down by our material self. We may feel that between our enfleshed finiteness and the infinite spirit of God there lies a gap, an abyss that we can never cross. We can sometimes, in moments of grace, come to the very edge of the gap, but that is as far as we can ever go.

Yet, if we are Christians, we also realize—not as an idea but as the reality of our faith—that in Christ the abyss has been raised, the gap has been bridged. In the Incarnation, Christ has entered the abyss; in his own body and soul he has joined the two sides once and for all. We have been joined with Christ, and in him we have been joined with God. Every moment of our lives, every event, every thought and every act, can become a sacrament of Divine presence in ourselves and in the world.

Incarnation is a belief that most of us have grown up with. It was probably presented to us when we were children, and we probably accepted it without much thought. Even as adults, we may not have cared enough to spend any time thinking on it. This belief was something we took on faith. Yet it is important to think of it, even to question it. Unless we do, we may never begin to realize the immensity of what the Incarnation tells us, not only about God, but also about ourselves: about who we really are.

When the true meaning of the Incarnation begins to penetrate our consciousness, we may find ourselves not only amazed but even shocked. For it tells us that, at one moment in history, God entered and took on the most basic, the least spiritual, level of human reality: its carnality, its flesh.[8] Not only did God in Christ enter a human body, which is a difficult enough idea to grasp; God entered our flesh and made it holy. God took on the raw material of the human reality and "divinized" it.

This event may seem shocking, because the flesh has had bad press among Christians. Most of us have probably been told in sermons or books that we must struggle to control our flesh, even to mortify it, to liberate ourselves from it. This attitude, fortunately, is no longer what our children or grandchildren tend to be taught, but it still persists in many minds. Flesh is still too often viewed as the body gone bad, identified with the wrong kind of desire, with sin, even with the devil himself.

But when the Bible speaks of the flesh, it seems to be referring not to any sinful tendencies or conditions of the body, but to the basic material, the matter, out of which our body is made—the clay or dust that God blessed and used to make us. The flesh is the body in its most fundamental meaning: our essential earthly or material aspect that we share with the whole of creation and that connects us to all creatures. The "way of all flesh" is the way of all finite, mortal beings: the way of life as well as of death.

If we reject or despise this essential element of our bodily nature, we reject the reality of who we are: human persons rooted in the material world. We open ourselves to the temptation to view ourselves as fundamentally—by nature—souls trapped in our own individual prison of flesh: forever forced to seek a way to escape from it, to overcome our dependence on the material world. If we reject and despise our flesh, we become foolish and unreal.

CLOSING OF THE CIRCLE

I t is, I believe, to teach us this great truth that Christ so often used matter—the physical element—in his teaching and in his life. His every action, every miracle, takes place in and is connected to the physical world. He spits on the ground and makes clay to restore the sight of the blind; he tells the leper or the paralytic to wash in the waters of the pool of Siloam in order to become healthy again. Christ turns plain, ordinary water into wine; he heals with his touch; he breathes on the sick; his voice calls forth the dead. And in the most "scandalous" of his acts, the most unacceptable teaching, he turns real bread and real wine into his own flesh and blood.

As we reflect on these events, we become aware that the material Christ uses is not irrelevant to the mystery he enacts, but rather expresses or symbolizes it. The clay out of which we were made, the saliva that heals, the water that cleans and restores, the bread of life, the wine red like the blood that courses in our veins: all point to the mystery inherent in the flesh.

As icon painters have always understood, every event of Christ's own life, his whole human experience, is an expression of this mystery. He is born in a cave, the most ancient and most primitive of human shelters, in the darkness of night, but in that darkness a great star burns in the heavens and the angels sing of his glory.[9]

At the Circumcision, he sheds his first blood and receives the name given to him by the angel: the name, a human word, through which the world is saved. When he is brought by his parents to be presented at the temple, old Simeon, filled with the Spirit, recognizes the greatness of the baby whose body he holds in his arms. At the beginning of his public life, Christ immerses his body in the waters of the Jordan, and the Spirit hovers over them, sanctifying them and making them a vessel of grace.

And, at the end, Christ's sacred flesh hangs on the cross made of wood and pours out his life's blood on the ground—the same ground out of which we were all formed—and saves the world. He dies and is laid in a tomb—another cave—and thus the circle of life and death, in which the whole human life is contained, is closed. But, on the third day, the rock splits open and Christ, his body glorious and whole again, rises from the tomb! The light of heaven fills the universe and the angels testify to his victory. The circle is broken and the finality of death is destroyed.

INCONCEIVABLE BELIEF

It is only when we begin to realize this fact of our total connection with Christ—body, mind and soul—that we can approach the Christian teaching on the resurrection of the body with some openness and understanding. One day, at the end of things, we are taught, our bodies—our own flesh—united with Christ's in an indissoluble bond, shall rise as his did, and thus with him and in him we shall be "glorified" and made one with God.

This belief is, and will always remain, inconceivable: our own minds could never have conceived of it. But neither could they have conceived of the Incarnation! It is a mystery and in this life at least we cannot understand or solve it. We need not, therefore, attempt to meddle with it or try to grasp it with our minds, but leave our hearts free to approach it with reverence and love.

This inconceivable belief has been part of Christian teaching from apostolic times. However difficult it might be for us to accept or to imagine, however wild it may appear to our modern, scientifically aware mind, we must not dismiss it out of hand. We cannot understand or imagine how this rising might happen, or what this mysterious resurrection body will be like, or how it will work. We can, it seems to me, safely assume that it will be very different from what we know as body in our earthly life.

For the body as we know it now cannot survive death: it cannot be "deathless." By its very nature, it is subject to change: it must be born, grow old and eventually die and thus return to earth, out of which it was made. And yet, as the early Christians clearly believed, it will be a body—different, transformed, shining with light, but still a body, not a ghost.

However we understand or interpret this vision of the new reality, we would do well to remind ourselves of the conviction that underlies everything said in this book: no teaching of the Christian tradition is ever meaningless or irrelevant to our own reality. Every teaching tells us something about ourselves as well as about God. From that perspective, belief in the resurrection of the body makes one important "fact" of our human reality clear. Our union with God, either in this life or in eternity, does not annul or dissolve our own individual personhood and our own individual awareness, as some religious traditions suggest. We shall not fall into God and disappear, like a river that flows into the ocean and ceases to exist.

Christian tradition has taught from the beginning that we shall remain ourselves—our own "I"—after death, just as Christ remained himself after his resurrection. He rose triumphant, glorified, so transfigured that he was not always easy to recognize, but still the same person: the Lord. If we become like him, if we live his life, if we are in communion with him while

73

we are on earth, we also shall be transformed, glorified, changed in a way we cannot even imagine, but
still the same person, a self.[10]

＊

ALWAYS OURSELVES

Some of us may find this tradition difficult to accept, not only because the belief in such a resurrected and deathless personal life seems to contradict all laws of nature and logic as we understand them, but also, perhaps, for more personal reasons. We may be tired of being ourselves and thus may not be happy at the prospect of an eternity of personhood.

For to be a person means to be unique—different from others—and therefore, in a fundamental way, alone, separated from others by outer and inner boundaries we cannot break. We might have preferred to have been created a little less unique! We may long, like the mystics, to lose ourselves in God.

To lose ourselves in God, however, does not necessarily mean to lose our selfhood or to sink our own being in the infinite being of God. The mystics may have wished for that at times, and described their experience in words that suggest such merging and loss of self. We, too, may have experienced such moments, perhaps in deep prayer or in a relationship of love, and think back to them with longing and hope.

But such moments pass and we emerge from them perhaps less lonely, more alive, but also more ourselves than we have ever been, although in a new, deeper, less defensive way. What we experience in these moments is not merging but *communion*: the opening of all doors, the letting down of all barriers. We are able just to be there, to be present to the one we love. This is as it must be. For only a self can be aware of another and enter into communion with another. Only a self can surrender to love. And if heaven is truly an eternity of love, it must also be a heaven of communion, of awareness and ceaseless self-surrender to God.

And yet we do not have to ignore or dismiss our longing for merging completely, for no human longing should be lightly ignored or dismissed. The heart is often wiser than the mind, and none of its deepest longings are totally mistaken, totally in vain. When it is open to the whole of reality, the heart may point to the truth that lies beyond any categories or definitions our minds may try to impose on it.

For when we at last become, as we are called to become, totally transformed into Christ, totally one with God for all eternity, how can we even begin to guess what our self or self-awareness will mean then? When Christ unites all things in himself and submits them all to God, what separateness can there be? What aloneness? In the eternity where time or place, or any other dimension known to the human mind, exist, how can we talk of any boundaries, any separation at all? What other awareness can there be but our awareness of God?

Still, in this life, this present reality, we need to recall that Christ, who reveals himself to us, is not just an impersonal, divine something of God imprinted on our hearts. He is not just another dimension or deeper level of our human reality. Christ is somebody: a person, a self. And thus, we can relate to him as persons. We can follow him and learn from him. We can get to know him and enter a relationship, a communion, with him.

KNOWING CHRIST

Getting to know Christ and entering into a relationship with him is the first essential step on our Christian way. Yet many of us may not be sure how to take that first step. The answer to the question of who Christ is cannot be found through studying books or learning it from others. It cannot be found by thinking *about* him, as if he were a theological or historical problem to solve. Knowing Christ is knowing him as we know a person we love, our closest friend. It is an encounter, a relationship of love.

This fact may take a little time to sink in, especially for those of us who tend to view all knowledge in terms of rational thought. We may find it very difficult to keep our minds from trying to figure Christ out, probing the mystery of his being with our rational minds and becoming disappointed and discouraged when we find the task impossible.

I experienced this danger when, soon after my return to the practice of Christianity, I went back to university to do some graduate work. One of my courses dealt with Church history from the third to the fifth centuries, during which several councils of the Church met to hammer out the Trinitarian teaching of Christianity.

Trying to understand what was involved in these debates about the nature of Christ and his relationship with the Father and why they had caused so much strife, including pitched battles in the streets, nearly brought me to despair. I wondered whether I was ready to take up the burden of this strange faith. The debates that aroused so much anger and even hate seemed so theoretical, so far from the realities of everyday Christian life! And yet they appeared vital not only to the Christians of those days, but to Christians of our own day as well.

My mind became taken up with all these questions; I agonized over them day and night. One afternoon, as I sat poring over my books and struggled to understand what it was all about, I must have dozed off. I dreamed that Christ came to visit me. I was overjoyed and said to him, "Please tell me, Lord, who are you really and what exactly is your relationship with the Father? Are you really God? I must know or I shall go mad!" But, instead of answering, Christ burst out laughing and said, "Have a heart, woman! Why don't you give me a cup of tea instead?"[11]

This dream was very significant for me. It helped me to realize how easy it was for me to fall into the illusion that I, or anyone else, could (or should try to) understand the mystery of Christ and make it totally clear and acceptable to my "thinking mind." It did not lead me to question or minimize the place of doctrinal teaching and theology in the Christian tradition. But it did help me to understand that these doctrines and definitions were not meant, at least originally, to be explanations of the mysteries of faith, but only signs that pointed to the realities that these mysteries expressed.

✳

MYSTERY OF LOVE

The most significant and most valid role that theology had played in the history of the Christian tradition, I realized, lay not in succeeding in the impossible task of explaining the mystery of God or of Christ in rational and philosophical terms, nor in setting up systems of doctrinal teaching, but in training the mind to know its own limitations and thus allowing it to approach the mystery with adoration and love. As Mother Maria once wrote with reference to the Mystery of the Holy Trinity,

> I think there is the very greatest help to us in our life on earth to know that there is something absolutely beyond us, a Mystery of love which we can only adore, of which our most eloquent witness is the deep silence of adoration, where mind and will are set at rest on a subject beyond their grasp...[12]

In order to know Christ, we do not have to be theologians or have a great intellect or deep insight. We don't have to be very pious or practise any extraordinary ways of prayer or life. We do not even have to be especially religious. As an Orthodox monk I know likes to say, Christianity is not a religion, but a way of living the life of heaven while still on earth.

In other words, Christianity is the life of communion and love.

Of course I did not understand this truth or stop agonizing over the mystery of Christ all at once. My questions and doubts remained. I felt at times that they would overwhelm me and that I might be losing my faith! Or that I had never found it in the first place.

I do not know where all this would have led me if I had not had the support and encouragement of some very good friends. One who was of special importance to me during those years was an old priest whom I saw often and asked for advice. He would never argue with me or try to convince me of anything. He would only listen to me patiently and then invariably say, "I have only three questions to ask you, and the first one is this: Do you love God?"

"Yes, of course, I love God," I would answer, "you know that I do!"

Then he would ask: "Do you love Christ?"

"I think I do," I would reply. "Why else would I go through all this misery?"

The third question was the most difficult. "Do you love your neighbour?"

"Not very well," I would have to tell him, "but I am trying to learn."

"In that case," he would declare, " there is nothing to worry about!" and send me away with a blessing and a hug. This did not really answer or explain my questions or doubts, but it put them in perspective; it made me laugh at myself a little and see the ridiculous side of my puny human mind trying to penetrate the infinite mystery of God's love manifested in Christ.

Christ, I began to see, was not difficult to approach. In order to find him, I did not have to know my catechism by heart. I did not have to struggle to understand arguments of theologians, or follow any mystical or esoteric path of wisdom, or practise any extraordinary ways of prayer or life. All I had to do was to love him in the best way I could, and occasionally offer him a cup of tea when he appeared at my door. But, first of all, I needed to learn to trust him enough to open the door!

*

THE WAY TO GOD

I t is at this point that I began to understand that the
true meaning of faith, in the biblical sense, is not
knowledge but trust. It is not about accepting this or
that doctrine. Thus, the Hebrews believed in God
and obeyed God's will not because they understood
the why of it, but because they trusted God's wisdom
and love. It is the lack of trust in God, in God's word
and promises, that made God "angry" at Israel.

The same understanding of faith is found in the
New Testament. As we read and ponder the Gospels,
we may be surprised to discover how little Christ
talked to his disciples about the nature of God or of
his own relationship with God. Christ told his disciples that he was the Son of God; that he came "from
the Father"; that those who saw him saw the Father,
also; that he and the Father were one. But he did not
explain to them what all these "facts" meant.

He did tell his disciples—and therefore us—over
and over again that they must trust God and trust
him—Christ—because he always did what God
willed him to do and said only what he had learned
from God. When he chided them for their "little
faith," he did so not because they failed to understand
who he really was, but because they failed to trust

him enough and would run away when the going got rough.

Christ did not come to replace the God of the Hebrews or nullify the need for any further search for God. He did not hand to us the whole solution to the mystery of God. He only pointed to himself and said, "I am the Way." In other words, Christ came to show us in his own person, in his own words and his own life and death, how we can find God who is beyond all concepts or images, beyond all human definitions or beliefs: who is unimaginable.

This is a fundamental principle of our faith that we must never forget. We search for Christ, we long to find him, we enter into a relationship with him not because he is the greatest, the most wonderful, the most kind and loving—and whatever other virtue we may think of—human being who has ever lived. We search for Christ and struggle to know and love him because, and only because, in him we encounter and recognize God. Christ is the Truth at the heart of all reality.

Christ is also the true and totally sufficient sacrament of the divine presence in us and among us. Christ himself is the greatest, the infinitely holy and powerful "mystery-event" always happening at the heart of reality. When we believe in him and join our lives with his, we, too, in our small human measure, become sacraments, vessels of the divine presence in the world.

Eventually, I came to terms with my own inability to understand the mystery of Christ and to be less worried by it. I realized that Christians do not need to be afraid of the fact that it is impossible for us ever to fully understand the nature of Christ in the way that our minds may still be craving: with an absolute certainty that would admit no shadow of doubt.

Doubt is unavoidable in the life of faith. Without ever questioning or doubting what we know (or think we know) about the teaching of our spiritual tradition, our faith could never grow. We could not clear away the layers of misconception and superficiality that our spiritual laziness—our sloth—has wrapped around the mystery of our salvation.

Doubt is the price we pay for having a mind, for being made free. For the essence of our faith in Christ lies not in understanding who he is so clearly, so completely, that we are compelled to believe in him: that it becomes impossible for us not to believe. The essence of faith is that it is free, that we choose to believe and trust him whom we cannot understand but whom we have encountered and love.

※

LOVE OF FRIENDS

When we think of love, what often comes first to our minds is the emotion of love: an emotional attachment to another. When we say we love someone, we may mean that we are emotionally involved with him or her, that we are "in love." We may also use the word *love* to express a dependency on others: a need for their presence and support at all times, a conviction that it would be impossible to live without them.

But love, as Christian teaching understands it, is not emotion but presence—not in the sense of physical presence, but rather in the sense of awareness and attention. When we truly love others, we are present to them as we are not able to be present to anybody else; we are always there for them; we stand by them in every need. In other words, to love another means to become their true friend.

Such friends are always with us—present to us—even when they are many miles away. We share with them our deepest thoughts and beliefs, our joys and pains, our hopes and fears. We often feel as if they were a real part of us, as if we were inseparable, as if we were one. We carry them, as we say, "in our hearts." We may not always understand our friends completely—we may even be hurt by and disappointed with them—but we do not judge them, we do not turn away from them. We love and forgive them.

We are there for our friends in their joy but also in their suffering and need. We may not be able to do anything for them or to relieve their sorrow or pain, but we are there for them. We offer them our compassion: we suffer with them.

This is not to deny the importance of emotion or need. Love, like every human experience, has roots in the flesh of our own desires and needs. To condemn any human love because it involves emotions would be to deny the reality of the human condition: that we are always dependent on others, on the world that surrounds us and, above all, on God. The struggle to love is not a struggle to get rid of emotion, but to move beyond it and find the heart of love that is awareness and presence.

There are many examples of such friendship in history and literature. Not surprisingly, most of the examples that have come down to us are of the heroic kind: stories of love and loyalty between two men, usually warriors who are companions in battle. But there were also other famous friendships: between men who search together for wisdom and truth (Plato considered such friendship the highest form of love) or between Christian monks searching for God. Friendships between women or between men and women, and there must have been many, remained mostly unsung.[13]

In our own age, the love of friendship is known and valued, but our understanding of it has changed. Our concept of love has become so bound up with sex that we often seem unable to imagine love and commitment between two persons without sex being involved. Yet sex does not need to be involved in the love of friends.

The heart of true friendship is not erotic love but love of deep affection, of understanding and mutual loyalty. True friendship is not based on possessive attachment but on mutual trust and respect. It is not exclusive, as erotic love tends to be; it does not close us off from others, but gives us the courage to trust ourselves enough to allow ourselves to be open to them. This is why the love of friendship seems to me the clearest image of the kind of love Christ has commanded us to have for one another. Also, I believe, it is the clearest image of the love between us and Christ.[14]

SHARING REALITY

To love a friend means to become so close, so attentive to him or her, that it may seem to us at times that we can truly enter our friend's heart: his or her true reality. The boundaries that separate us from each other—the boundaries of our uniqueness, our personal histories, our different emotional and psychological needs, our differences of ideas and even of religious beliefs—disappear for a moment and we are truly one.

As I write this, I am thinking of a moment of such sharing I once experienced with my friend Renee. Renee and I met during our first year of college and have remained close ever since. Both of us came from Poland at more or less the same time. We both had lived through the war and occupation (although we did not know it, we even lived in the same town for a few months). We both had experienced life under Communism, escape to the West, arrival in a new country, learning a new language, building a new life.

There was, however, a gap between us, a dividing line, that separated us from each other: Renee was Jewish and I was not. We had lived in and escaped from two different realities. We had, of course, always known that this gap existed, but hardly ever talked about it in the early years of our friendship. We were perhaps too busy with life and too close in many other ways to bother much with our past. Or maybe we preferred not to talk about it because on some level of our minds we knew that, if we did, we might find it too painful and too difficult to handle.

It was only years later, during one of my visits from Canada, that we began to speak about it. One evening, as we talked late into the night, she told me what the war had been like for her. Renee, like me, was eight when the war began. She told me how she and her mother moved from one place to another under assumed names and false documents. She described their fear and their sense of constant danger of betrayal and death. How every few weeks or months someone would look at them closely, sometimes with compassion but often with indifference or hostility, perhaps even threatening to report them to the German police. And so they would run again, move to another town, pretend to be someone else, yet always remain on their guard.

I had heard similar tales before, but they had never seemed quite real. They were just horrible stories from the past. But now, as I listened to my friend in the dark, I was overcome with a feeling of horror and shame (for how could I be sure how I would have behaved towards her had I met her in those days?). And yet, at the same time, I also experienced such a profound sense of being *there* with her, of sharing her life and her fear, that for that moment at least, her reality truly became my own.[15]

The experience did not remain vivid for long, but I have never forgotten it. I have never quite lost the sense of what I understood then: not only about Renee's life, but also about the meaning of love, of trust, of being truly present and open to a friend's reality.

✳

EXTREME COMMAND

C hristians, however, are called to an even greater love. We are called to love and forgive not only those who love and understand us, whose lives we share with joy, but our enemies as well. For, as Christ said, even the "pagans" love their friends (Matthew 5:47). Those of us who claim to be his disciples must struggle to love those who hate us and do us harm.

Christ's command to love our enemies has caused many Christians endless inner struggle and doubt. How can we forgive those who have hurt us or hurt our family and friends? How can we avoid judging them? How can we stop feeling angry towards them or afraid of them? Do we have no right to defend ourselves and others from harm? What purpose would "forgiveness" of such people serve?

To forgive our enemies does not mean condoning or forgetting the evil they have done; it does not mean not trying to prevent them from committing it, or letting them go free to commit it again. In every human society, the innocent must be protected and the evildoer must be contained and prevented from doing more harm.

Nor does loving our enemies mean forcing ourselves to acquire any tender feelings towards those who have done us harm. It does not mean denying that they have done us wrong. It does not mean absolving them from the necessity of repenting for their crimes or from having to face the consequences of their acts. Even God will not do those things.

To love and forgive our enemies means refusing to allow the evil they have done to us to infect our own hearts and lives with its poison, and thus to spread it further in the world. It means refusing to hate them or to seek revenge on them, however hurt or angry we may feel. It also means being willing to give them another chance to repent and change, if it is reasonable to expect such a change and if it does not put the safety of others at risk.

In other words, to love and forgive our enemies means trying to put our hurts and anger aside—not denying that we have been hurt, but refusing to act out of our hurt. It means trying to see those who hate us as God sees them: mean and cruel, perhaps, needing to be stopped from doing further harm, and yet each a human being, one of those whom Christ has told us to love.

Such love may not make much sense to us at first. For a long time, it did not make much sense to me. It seemed not only impossible to achieve, but also unnatural to attempt. I could not forget the real evil I had witnessed and experienced as a child. I could not forget the damage it had done to so many lives. It is ironic, perhaps, that the person who helped me most to understand such "unnatural" love was Renee's husband, Dante, who, like Renee, had experienced the horror of the Holocaust, and who had lost all of his family and much of his health as a result.

※

VICTORY OF LOVE

D ante was an artist who, although he belonged to no religion, was truly aware of the divine presence that could be found behind every form and in every expression of earthly reality. "All great art," he used to tell me, "is religious." Whenever I was in London, we would go to the galleries and museums together. There he taught me what he could about the way he understood art. He taught me to stand in front of a work of art and just look at it: not to think of anything, not to say anything, but just to look. We would talk about what we had seen only after we got back home.

During my last visit, a year before his death, he was already too ill to come with me, so I went alone. But he gave me an assignment. I was to go to the National Gallery and look at *Christ Mocked* (*Crowning with Thorns*) by Hieronymus Bosch. I was to ask myself with which one of the four tormentors of Christ I could best identify, with whom I felt most akin. I was rather taken aback by this assignment, but I knew him well and I trusted him, and anyway he was too sick to be argued with. So I went. I stood a long time before the painting and looked.

After a while I remembered the question Dante had told me to ask and I was shocked, even frightened, to realize that I could identify with all four tormentors! I was familiar with their coldness and cruelty, for I had experienced these in my own life and in myself. I understood the way they looked at Christ, the way they touched him, their jeering faces full of hate. It was only Christ who was totally unfamiliar to me, with whom I could not identify at all.

I saw his quiet face, his body totally relaxed, without any sign of the withdrawal that every human being must surely feel when touched and seized by such ugly and cruel hands, when spat upon, beaten and crowned with thorns. I felt angry at him for being so defenceless and passive, so seemingly unconcerned.

How could he stand there, so silent and unresponsive to the way they treated him? Why did he, who had performed miracles and claimed a power greater than any magician or saint had ever claimed, who could have called on "more than twelve legions of angels" to come to his side (Matthew 26:53), allow such evil to go unresisted and unpunished?

I went back and told Dante how I felt. "Go back," he said, "and look again." It was during my second or third visit that I began to understand what the painting was telling me. I saw the immense power of Christ's apparent passivity. To allow himself to be so treated, so touched by wicked men without cringing, without any sign of hate, was not to be passive but to be truly active and free! Christ did not lose his power but put it aside. He was then, as he has always been, sovereign and free. He had won his victory over evil with love.

NEGATION OF REALITY

When we think of evil, we often think of it in terms of darkness and light. We think of Christ coming to conquer the darkness of evil with his own divine light, thus freeing us from its power. That is a powerful and useful image: we could hardly talk about evil without it. But it is only an image, and should not be pushed too far. For evil and darkness are not synonymous.

Darkness, the absence of light, is not evil. It is a natural part of created reality, just as night and day are. If there were no darkness, there would be no light; if the sun never set, it could never rise again. Darkness and light are two sides of the same reality.

In the same way, we might also think of evil in terms of the suffering and pain it brings. Suffering can be, and often is, the result of an evil act and sometimes even its cause, but in itself is not evil. Suffering is part of the reality of our life on earth. Christ, in whom there was no evil, bore it for our sake. He entered the fullness of human suffering in order to show us that it was not evil; that God was as present to us in suffering as God is in every other aspect of reality.

We do not understand why it must be so. We might and often do rebel against it, or are angry at God for it, and yet it is so. Nothing we can do—no invention or miracle cure—can remove suffering from our world for good. Suffering exists; it is real.

Evil, on the other hand, is a total negation of reality. The definition of evil is not that it is painful and dark or even unreal, but that it is *anti*-real: the enemy of reality and thus the enemy of God. It is a rejection of God: a total refusal to accept the reality as it was created by God. Evil is also an antithesis of love. Its root is hate: the desire to pervert and destroy what God has made.[16]

Existence of evil, even more than the existence of suffering, is not easy to understand or accept. Faced with the immensity of evil that torments the world we live in, we may begin to doubt both the infinite love and the infinite power of God. We cannot comprehend how God could have ever allowed evil to enter and destroy the lives of so many human beings.

In the Christian tradition, however, evil is always viewed as an enemy or perversion of reality, and thus not the will of God. The biblical story of the Fall illustrates that belief. Evil is the curse that humanity has borne from the moment when our first parents looked at themselves through the eyes of the Enemy and despised and rejected their own true reality. It was then, according to Christian teaching, that evil first entered the world (Genesis 3).

*

THE HOLLOW MEN

To believe that human beings may and often do evil things does not mean to believe that they can ever become totally evil, totally unreal. For, if they did, they would cease to exist. A totally evil person would have no reality at all, would have no being, and thus could not *be*.

There are human beings, however, who seem to have come very close to that "nonexistence." They are the "hollow men," as T.S. Eliot called them, those who hate reality so much that they spend most of their lives trying to destroy and pervert it in themselves, in others and in the world. They are those who may seem to us "possessed" by evil, "stuffed" with emptiness.

Most of us do not reject or hate God. But we do not always experience God as the core of our reality. We do not really seek God, we are not aware of God, we have little room for God in our lives. We often live our daily lives as if there were no God.

Neither do we hate our own reality so totally that we want to destroy it. Yet many of us, if not most, may find it impossible to embrace it totally, all the time. We may want to escape or even deny it. We try to create our own version of it—a false self—and impose it on others. Although we are not evil, we become tainted with unreality.

Evil has wrought endless suffering and pain in the world. It has distorted and destroyed countless human lives. And yet, Christ—who, we are taught, came to "save the world from evil"—did not banish it from the world any more than he banished all suffering. Christ, to whom "all power on earth and in heaven" had been given (Matthew 28:18), could have done so, but he did not. It is often difficult for us to understand why.

There can be only one explanation of this painful truth: God had given us the freedom to embrace or rebel against the reality he had made, and Christ would not undo what God had done: he would not take our freedom away.

This is a terrifying and debilitating truth to realize and live with, but it is only one side of the truth. For, if it is true that the consequences of every evil act are always with us, so are the consequences of all the good that is ever done. Not one act of mercy or love will ever fail to bear fruit. Evil will not overwhelm the good. This is the fundamental hope and promise of the Christian faith.

But it is not our only hope. For although evil can never be undone, it can be healed. Its consequences, the wounds it inflicted, can be healed as Christ heals them: by forgiveness and love. As evil is the antithesis of love, so is love the antithesis of hate. It is an antidote to hate.

Such healing may not come right away—the wounds may hurt and fester for many years, even for centuries—yet sooner or later they will be healed by someone's forgiveness and love. Love is the "divine alchemy" that can turn the terror and hate that evil has caused into good.

The call to struggle with evil in our own lives is a call to open our hearts to the power of this "alchemy" and to allow it to transform our human hearts into channels of Christ's own healing love. It is a call to receive as much—or as little—of his compassion and love as our hearts can absorb, and to pass it on to those who are sent our way.

✳

IMPOSSIBLE TASK

When we begin to have even a glimpse of the cost of such love, we soon realize that it is indeed impossible for us to achieve. No human love could ever approach the infinite love of God that Christ came to reveal. This self-evident fact should not surprise or discourage us. For we are not asked to equal Christ in loving. We are asked only to share, in some small measure, in what he has already done, what he has already achieved. We are asked only to open ourselves to Christ's love and let it heal our hearts and teach us how to love.

This is not an easy task. Even in the most loving human relationships, there are always limits to how much love we can and want to accept; how much we are prepared to open ourselves to others; how much we want to be known. There is usually a point in loving beyond which we are not prepared to go, at which we begin to count the cost. For we know—perhaps not consciously, but we know—that to love unconditionally means that, sooner or later, we shall have to pull down the defences and walls we have built around ourselves and feel compelled to maintain. Sooner or later, love will break through those walls and strip us naked.

We are not always aware of these disguises and defences, nor are we able to understand why we build and maintain them. What is it that we fear so much to acknowledge or admit to others? If we are aware of them, we may see them as necessary, a way to protect ourselves from being judged and rejected by others, as we believe has happened in the past and fear might happen again.

We may blame our parents, our teachers, society, the Church or a million other persons or institutions for our fear. We may feel that they have never loved us, but rejected us and betrayed our trust. This may well be true; we may have been treated in a way that has made it very difficult, and at times impossible, to trust and open ourselves to others. We may need much love and support, perhaps even professional help, before we are able to let go of our fear.

But it is not only others who may reject us. We may reject ourselves, blaming ourselves for what no one else has—or should never have—blamed or rejected us for: weaknesses that we were born with, consequences of events and genetic factors that are no fault of our own. We may dislike and despise ourselves for being imperfect and weak, perhaps even crippled or malformed, and thus essentially unlovable. How can we believe that anyone can truly love and accept us? Those who think they do love us are surely making a dreadful mistake, and we must never let them find it out.

It should not surprise us to discover that it may be even more difficult, and at times impossible, for us to open ourselves to Christ's love. We are afraid (perhaps not consciously, but still afraid) that if we allow ourselves to become so completely open and known to him in whom there is no shadow of imperfection or sin, he may turn away from us in horror and reject us like everyone we have ever loved seems to have done. This is a truly terrifying temptation that we must resist with all our strength. It is a manifestation of the primeval guilt: the fear of our own reality, the curse of the Fall.

CHRIST WILL TEACH US

It is from this fear and this temptation that Christ has come to deliver us. Christ has known and loved us long before we were born. He is always aware of us and present to us, every moment of our lives. All our disguises and illusions cannot prevent him from knowing and loving us. Christ loves us infinitely; he is the infinite love of God made flesh. He cannot *not* love us. Even to suspect otherwise is a sure sign of how little we really understand and know him, and how little he means to us.

And yet, most of us, I believe, have had moments when we did experience his presence so clearly, when we were so aware of him being there, at the heart of our reality, that we could not doubt his love. We need to remember these moments and hold onto our trust that they were not an illusion, but real. Christ is with us and in us, always open to us and loving us. All we need to do is to keep on struggling with our fear and mistrust and try to be aware of his presence and open to his love.

Nobody can really teach us how to become aware of Christ's presence and open to his love. Even the greatest of saints could not teach us that, for it is not a lesson we can learn from others. We must learn it by ourselves; we must search for it and keep searching and refuse to be defeated by our fears and doubts.

Yet, although nobody can teach us how to be aware of Christ's presence, we can, and sometimes must, be helped by others: an experienced spiritual guide, a friend or a community of friends. They can show us, by their acts and their presence rather than their words, that Christ's love is real. They can point out a path or a way of prayer that they have found helpful and encourage us to try it.

They can reassure and support us when we think we are getting nowhere, when Christ seems as absent and as far away as always, when we become despondent, overwhelmed by doubt. Helping others to find their own path of knowing and loving Christ is the most important ingredient of Christian spiritual guidance.

It is not easy, however, to find such guidance in our world. We must often set out on our search alone. Yet this is no excuse for not setting out or for giving up. Christ is always with us, closer to us than any human teacher can ever be. He has taken us on (or we would not have begun to search for him in the first place) and at some point he himself will show us how to become aware of his presence and open ourselves to it.

Christ will send us circumstances that will make it easier or more compelling for us to set out on our search, and companions who will share it with us, support us and sometimes even drag us along when we feel like giving up. But Christ may also send us enemies—most often those who live within our own minds and hearts—who will not leave us in peace and will never let us forget how weak and fearful we are, how desperate is our need for healing that only Christ can bring.[17]

Christ will teach us how to find him in every relationship, in every event and every moment of our lives. His love may leap out at us in the most unexpected places, in the darkest hours of our lives. He will teach us that to become truly aware of reality, even of the smallest particle of it, is to become aware of him whom heaven and earth cannot contain, who fills all things and yet is always with us and in us, present in our hearts.

Our search may take time; it may bring us much doubt, disappointment and pain. Yet, if we persevere, our hearts will eventually learn to recognize him and will "burn within us" at his presence, wherever and however they find it. We shall realize that Christ has been with us all along the way. We shall learn to love and trust him like the Apostles, and all his disciples ever since, have loved and trusted him: as our true Master, Teacher and Friend.

※

THE TEACHER

It is difficult for us to understand what a teacher or guru meant in the ancient world and still means in some religious traditions. To most of us, a religious teacher means someone who is able and qualified to pass on a system of religious knowledge and morality. If we are lucky enough to find such a teacher, we think of him or her as our spiritual guide and friend. We talk to our teacher about our spiritual life and the problems we encounter on it, and ask for advice.

But to be a true teacher or master, as most spiritual traditions understand it, means something greater than being a spiritual guide and friend. True spiritual teachers do much more than instruct us in a particular way of prayer, or guide us on a particular spiritual path. Their main task is not to lead us to any higher wisdom or virtue, but only to God. In the Christian tradition, that means to lead us to Christ.

The most powerful image of a true teacher can be found at the beginning of the New Testament, in John the Baptist, the Forerunner of Christ. John insists that he himself is not the Messiah, but only the "voice crying in the wilderness." He was sent into the world to prepare the people for the coming of the One who would "baptize them with the Holy Spirit and fire" (Matthew 3:11).

This coming is not to be a gentle, non-disturbing event but an event of power, a wake-up call. "He will hold his winnowing fan in his hand. He will clear his threshing floor and gather his wheat into his barn, but the chaff he will burn with unquenchable fire" (Matthew 3:12). The Messiah is the "Lamb of God," to be crucified by the world's blindness and sin, but also the Lord who conquers all evil and unreality and sin. He is the true Teacher come into our world to show us the way to truth.[18]

Yet even Christ, for all his power and all his love, cannot make us learn what we do not want to learn, face what we do not want to face, or go where we do not want to go. Christ is the Way, but he cannot force us to walk it. He cannot make us become his disciples; he cannot, and will not, make us love him and give our lives over to him. He will not force us to follow him. We may, and often do, refuse.

But he also might, and probably will, place us in a situation or bring us to a point in our lives when we must decide to say "yes" or "no" to him and accept whatever consequences our decision may bring. The decision may not always be taken consciously, expressed in any clear thought or words. It may be an act, a turning, an irretrievable step that commits us to follow him or turn away.

✳

DECISION·FOR CHRIST

The finality and suddenness of the summons to a decision that we find in the Gospel accounts of Christ's call of his first disciples have always fascinated and rather frightened me. They met him; they glimpsed him in passing, or he looked at them; and they left whatever they were doing, whatever had been most important to them till that moment, and followed him (see Mark 1:16-20 and John 1:35-50).

As I write this, I am reminded of a dream a friend once told me about. She dreamt that she was standing at a window of a train that had stopped at a station unknown to her. The conductor had already blown his whistle and was banging the carriage doors shut when she noticed a small, unimpressive man dressed in a dark suit walking on the platform near the end of the train.

She could not see him well, but was sure she had never seen him before. And yet, at that moment, she knew she had to meet him; she had to get off the train immediately, before it left. But then she recalled the luggage she had with her, the friend she was going to visit, the life that she had worked hard to make for herself and that she enjoyed. She knew that if she got off the train she would never regain any of these things. She was torn by agonizing indecision. Then she woke up. "Ever since then," she said, "I have not stopped wondering what I would have done if I had not woken up."

Neither my friend nor I considered ourselves Christians at the time, and did not think of the person she saw from the train in Christian terms, but only as some truly "enlightened" spiritual master or guru who would show her the way to truth. But, in the years since I returned to Christianity, I have often thought of my friend's dream and how well it expressed what the decision to become a disciple of Christ has come to mean to me.

Most of us do not experience our decision in such dramatic terms. We may begin to follow Christ half-heartedly at first, perhaps just obscuring him from a distance, hanging around at the edge of the crowd. We may try to postpone the final commitment as long as we can. But, in the end, this is what it always comes down to: a moment of irrevocable choice. The choice is presented to us from outside of ourselves: as a challenge, a grace that we have done nothing to deserve and even, perhaps, have not asked for. But the response is always ours to give, and it must always be given freely. The decision must come from us. The call to follow Christ is an invitation to love, and love, like trust, is always free. It must come from within: from the truth of our own being, our own heart.

I wonder if we reflect on this aspect of our tradition often enough. We may be too apt to think of Christ's call in terms of one specific way of following him. Perhaps we believe that to be truly his disciples we must choose one special vocation, live one kind of "Christian life," pray in one special way, or follow one special devotion. In other words, we imagine that we must all fit into one pattern of discipleship—and that often means our own.

☀

WHICH CHRIST?

B ut there is no set pattern of discipleship. We do not have to force ourselves or allow others to force us into seeing and following Christ in a way that others choose to follow him, love him as others love him, or imagine him as others imagine him. We need not be afraid of experiencing his presence and responding to his call in the way that speaks most clearly to us, even if no one else understands it or approves of it.

This aspect of Christ's teaching, it seems to me, is reflected in the different ways the four Gospels present Christ to us. When we read carefully their accounts of the life and teaching of Christ, we soon become aware of this divergence. They differ not only in the way they describe some of the events or sayings of Jesus, or in the context or order in which these things are placed. These differences are well known to scholars and apparently not too difficult for them to reconcile.

The differences between the Gospels may go much deeper than these details. At times, it may even seem that we are presented with four distinct images of Christ: not necessarily contradictory, but different. This can be most clearly seen in the way the image of Christ of the Gospel of John varies from that presented by the three synoptic Gospels (Matthew, Mark and Luke), and even, although to a lesser degree, in the way the latter three differ from each other.

When I first noticed this apparent incongruity, I was surprised and a little disconcerted. How was I to know which Christ was the true one? Which one was I to believe in and follow? Which one was I to love?

Eventually, I realized that there was no incongruity; the different accounts do not undermine but rather complement each other. The fact that so soon after Christ's death each Evangelist saw and heard his Master in his own individual way and that all four were accepted and revered by the Christian community seemed no longer alarming but reassuring to me. It helped me to understand what Christians seem to have later forgotten, that there is no one exclusive way to know and love Christ; each one of us is called to find him and follow him in the way that seems most true to us. The truth of Christ is big enough to contain and reflect the truth of us all.

This is why most of us have a favourite Gospel: one that makes Christ more present to us, where we feel we can encounter and love him a little more easily. My favourite Gospel, the one I love and read most often—the one that makes my heart "burn" more easily—is the Gospel of John. But how much poorer the Church would be, and how much poorer my own faith would be, if there had been no other Gospel passed down to us.

I am convinced that to seek and follow Christ in a way that is not really our own—that does not reflect our own truth—would not only be pointless, but might even be dangerous to us and to others. For if we do not respect our own truth, how can we respect the truth of others? Why would we hesitate to impose our own ideas and beliefs on them? Is this not how fanatics and persecutors are made? Fanatics are not recruited from those who know and respect their own inner freedom, but from those who do not—those who must violate the freedom of others in order to reassure themselves that their own faith is real.

✳

ACCEPTING OURSELVES

To say that in order to know and love Christ we must embrace and follow him in our own way—the way that is true to our own reality—does not mean we have the right to believe and do what we want, to pick and choose our own brand of Christianity or set up our own rules of behaviour. If we are to be disciples of Christ, then we must do what our Teacher has called us to do; we must embrace and follow his teaching as well as we can. But each one of us must embrace and follow it in the way that is true to us: that expresses our own deepest truth.

And here, I believe, lies the greatest challenge of our spiritual lives: we do not really know how to be true to ourselves, or even what being true to ourselves means. We do not know how to love and trust ourselves in the simple, uncomplicated way that small children accept themselves before they are taught otherwise. We need to remind ourselves that being imperfect and weak does not disqualify us from being beloved in the eyes of Christ. When we are in his presence, we do not have to hide or pretend.

We need to learn that our far-from-perfect self, which we have such difficulty loving and accepting, has been created by God to play a part—perhaps a very small and yet an essential part—in incarnating a little bit of Christ in the world. We must therefore accept *all* of ourselves—the perfect and the imperfect—with respect and gratitude.

I had a very clear and moving example of this point recently at the funeral of an old lady I had known for years, or so I thought. She was a very quiet person, physically and emotionally somewhat disabled, yet she always seemed peaceful and kind. And so I was surprised by the story that a priest told us at her funeral. She had had a very difficult and loveless childhood, he said, and developed many emotional and physical problems after she grew up.

As a young adult, she had a mental breakdown and had to be hospitalized. For days, she lay on her bed silent and withdrawn. But one night, a nurse heard her whispering her prayers to God, thanking and praising him for all the problems and handicaps he had given her to bear. The nurse asked her later what her prayer had meant. "I praised God for my handicaps, because they taught me how to find him and love him," she replied.

I was deeply touched by this story, for it helped me to understand more clearly what it means to accept and love our own reality. Our reality, our true self, is wonderful and holy, however dissatisfied we may be with it and however obsessively we try to hide it from others. It is not perfect, but it has been given to us by God and has all we need to become fully the self we were created to be.

The deepest foundation of Christian love—for God, for others, but also for ourselves—rests on the conviction that our small, individual realities are embraced and brought together in Christ, whose reality is the full human expression of the ultimate reality of God. If we fail to embrace our own reality, we fail to embrace the reality of God.

God's divine reality is reflected in us, although only partially: as the sun is reflected in a drop of water or in a splinter of broken glass. Or, as St. Thérèse of Lisieux would say, we are only a little cup that God's infinite life fills to the brim. Each of us can contain only a tiny bit of this life, but it is God's life and so we are all filled. Our cup overflows and the world becomes a little more holy, a little more real.

Here, we may begin to see more clearly why our path to Christ must also be a path of self-knowledge. We seek to know ourselves—every aspect of our reality—because it is the only way we can free ourselves from our self-illusions and fear, find our true heart and encounter Christ who lives there. Without Christ—God in us—as our final end, we cannot understand and truly love ourselves. To know Christ and to know ourselves are not two separate paths, but one.

✳

THE COST OF DISCIPLESHIP

For most of us, this path is a very difficult one. We may not even be sure that we want to take it. There are too many layers of unreality wrapped around ourselves that we must strip off, too many defences to break down, too much fear to overcome. We may have been disliking and hiding our true self for so long—our "false self" that we have created for ourselves may have become so familiar to us—that we are convinced it is all we are or can be, and that to "give it up" would destroy us.

And yet, if we want to be the disciples of Christ, we must begin to walk the path he has shown us. The main task of a Christian, our own part in Christ's work of salvation, is to dispel the darkness and fear of self-illusion and unbelief in our own hearts. We cannot follow Christ unless we are willing to become real both with him and with ourselves.

We are very fortunate if we begin this work early in life. This does not happen very often; we have too much at stake, too much fear. It demands from us to attempt what we have struggled for many years to avoid: to let go of all our disguises and to strip ourselves of all our unreality. It may be only later in life that we realize the mortal danger that threatens us if we do not take up the task: the danger of never knowing who we really are, never finding our true heart and discovering the true meaning of ourselves.

But however early or late we come to that point, however deeply we understand our need of discovering the truth of ourselves, we cannot avoid facing the question that may seem unanswerable to us at first: How can we become truly ourselves, truly real, if we do not even know or have forgotten what "being real" means? How can we find our true heart if we have never learned what it is?

This is a question to which there is no one definite answer. There is no formula for being ourselves. There has never been another person like us, so our reality cannot be compared with anyone else's. We cannot discover it by thinking or by analyzing ourselves. We cannot find it defined in the Bible or in the teaching of the Church.

Neither is there (or at least I have never discovered it) a spiritual way of finding the meaning of our own real "self" in one single moment of enlightenment or insight. For although we may have had a few moments' intuition, a few glimpses of who we really are, they soon passed, our "enlightenment" grew dim, and we were again left face to face with our unreality and fear.

It is often only after much disappointment and doubt that we begin to realize that our constant lapses back into unreality do not need to make us afraid. We need not panic that we are irrevocably lost and shall never find the truth of ourselves. As long as we hold on to our trust in Christ, as long as we try to be real, our lapses are not mere obstacles but may become stepping stones to truth. Our constant, patient work of uncovering and letting go of all that is not true, not real in us, is our true path to reality, however painful and discouraging it may seem at times.

Our life with Christ cannot come easy or cheap. He will indeed winnow all that is chaff from us so that only the wheat remains. Christ did give us fair warning. He did say that only the brave may enter the Kingdom; that to find it we must give away all that we have, everything we cling to and hide ourselves behind. We must give away all our possessions—not only material ones but, perhaps more importantly, all other riches we cling to: our pride, our need for control, our illusions of greatness. We may even have to give up our lives. To be a disciple of Christ means a kind of death.

✳

GOD IS A TIGER

When I was still searching for a way to God, I was willing to go anywhere, learn from anybody, try anything. I studied various religions and read books by countless spiritual gurus and masters. I explored many spiritual paths. But I was never satisfied, never at peace.

A friend who knew me well used to become exasperated with me and my attempts at "finding God." "For heaven's sake, woman!" he once shouted (he was much given to shouting and waving his arms if excited). "So, you are looking for God? And who do you think God is? A pussycat you can play with? God is a tiger, and if you manage to find him one day you might not like it at all!"

"Don't be so dramatic," I told him. "What do you think God will do to me?"

"He will tear you to pieces!" my friend replied.

I have often thought of that conversation and how accurate my friend's dramatic warning has turned out to be. For although God, whom I had found in Christ, was as merciful and full of forgiveness as I had hoped, his mercy was not always gentle. God was a tiger who allowed his own son to be "torn to bits," stripped of everything, even his life, to show us the way we too must follow to find the fullness of life.

When we find Christ and strive to become his disciples, we soon find out that he is not likely to let us cling to anything that obstructs us on the way. However loving, gentle and merciful he may be with us, however accepting of our weakness and fear, he will not let us be lost in our unreality for long. He will soon insist that we begin to strip ourselves not only of our sins, but of all that is not true, not real.

I discovered this for myself soon enough. When I returned to Christianity I believed, or rather deluded myself, that now, because I had found Christ, all my inner struggles and failures were over. I thought all my wounds would be healed and God would cancel all the consequences of my mistakes and my sins. I would become kind and loving and prayerful all at once.

I was soon disappointed, however, for it became quite clear—to myself and to everybody else, especially my family—that I was not becoming any holier or wiser than I was before. I was not becoming any more patient, any more accepting of myself or others, nor, I suspect, any easier to live with. I was not able to love and accept myself any better than I did before. I still had to ask for forgiveness for the same weaknesses and sins over and over again.

Neither did I seem to be developing any kind of special relationship with Christ. Although I was still praying the Jesus Prayer as often as I could, I had not (nor have I since) managed to pray it or any other prayer "well," to sit still and silence my ever-chattering mind for more than a few seconds or to stick to any schedule or rule of prayer. I have never managed to pray attentively—with awareness—for long. From every aspect I could see, I was forced to consider myself a total failure at spiritual life.

✳

JOINING THE SINNERS

All these failures and disappointments worried me a lot at first. What I was doing wrong? Were goodness and love always to be out of reach? Would I never relax and become less dissatisfied with myself and with the world? Would I ever learn how to pray well? Had I misunderstood how I should practise the Jesus Prayer, or was I not meant to pray it?

I used to talk to the priest who first introduced me to the prayer about my problems and fears (many times, poor man) and ask him for help. He would only grin at me and say, "It is not easy to join us sinners, eh? But have courage, you will manage it one day." And, in the end, after much confusion and pain, I did.

I saw that the practice of the Jesus Prayer, or any other way of real prayer, had little to do with acquiring an exceptional degree of holiness or wisdom and being freed once and for all from all our weaknesses and sins. For me at least, it seemed to be a way of constant failure, of having to face again and again my own lack of love, my fear of rejection and my attempts to escape from reality: a way of realizing how little I had learned of Christ's teaching, how poorly I knew him and how little I knew myself.

But as I kept trying to pray the Jesus Prayer, regardless of how disappointed I felt with my own efforts and my whole inner life, I had a glimmer of hope. If these poor efforts were all I could make, then I would make them and put all my trust only in Christ. This, I believe, was the greatest grace that the Jesus Prayer bestowed on me: I never became completely discouraged, never quite ready to give it up. I was determined that if I could not pray it "well," I would pray it "badly." In fact, praying it badly became, in a rather extraordinary way, an essential and constructive aspect of my spiritual life. It forced me to understand more clearly and focus more fully on the significance of the second half of the prayer: the call for mercy. I began to say the words "have mercy on me, a sinner!" with far greater conviction and hope.

Like most contemporary Christians, I found it difficult to feel comfortable with the notion of being a sinner. I was aware, of course, that I had often committed wrong, perhaps even evil, acts: I have broken the commandments and needed to repent and make amends. I had often failed at being kind or loving or forgiving enough. I was not always faithful in fulfilling my duties; I did not always tell the truth. Yet the notion of being a sinner all the time—being defined as a sinner and having to repent for it—did not seem reasonable to me. Rather, it seemed to be an expression of a very gloomy and judgmental view of human nature that I had never found convincing or appealing.

But now I realized that praying so constantly, so insistently, for mercy, I was repenting for more than any specific sins I may have committed. I was not accusing myself of being evil—of being "stuffed with evil"—but acknowledging that I, like all human beings, was tainted with it. I too had turned away—had become alienated—from God and from my own reality again and again.

It was this state of alienation that early Christian teachers referred to as "the sin of Adam" or "the human condition." When we ask for mercy, we are not rejecting our own true reality but asking Christ to help us find it. We are asking him to make us aware of all our alienation and teach us how to let go of it. And so, we realize, we have discovered the ancient Christian path of conversion: the path of becoming truly real by facing our unreality and stripping ourselves of it—repenting of it—bit by bit.[19]

✳

A LIFETIME'S WORK

Conversion may be an event of major significance, a return after many years or even a lifetime of selfishness and sin. But it can also be a return from a short lapse into unreality, or even from a mere moment of inattention, of becoming distracted and lost in our thoughts or emotions, away from the presence of God. We may be saying the words of the prayer, calling on the name of Christ, when we realize that our minds have strayed, our feelings are in turmoil, we have become absent from Christ and from ourselves; we have forgotten who we truly are.

As soon as we realize it, however, we "wake up" and return to the presence. We remember that Christ is in us and with us: infinitely more aware of us than we ever succeed in being aware of ourselves, more merciful perhaps than we have expected or hoped for. We relax and begin to see ourselves as Christ sees us: accepted and loved just as we are. The moment of absence has brought us even closer to Christ.

This, I think, is true of any practice of prayer we undertake. For every true prayer—every prayer that comes from the heart—is a return, an entrance into the presence of God. It is a *metanoia*, a change or turning of the heart, as the early Greek saints called it. Every time we return our attention to Christ and enter his presence again, we return to our true reality. His mercy covers us and we are at peace.

As the years pass and I become more comfortable with myself, less bothered by my imperfections and less frightened by my sins, I see that Christ's mercy is much more than his pity for our weakness or his willingness to forgive our sins. Christ's mercy is his never-failing presence in us and with us, whether we know it or not, whether we deserve it or not, and even whether we ask for it or not.

Christ's mercy is the presence of someone who is filled with compassion and total acceptance of us as we are; who does not condemn or reject us when we sin; who does not abandon us when doubts assail us and we think we are lost; who does not forget us when we are afraid or in pain but stays and suffers with us through it all.

To ask for mercy is to ask for love. It is to approach someone we love and trust totally, someone who loves us and knows us as we cannot ever love or know ourselves, who sees all our unreality and sin, and yet does not turn away from us even for a moment—someone who is always there.

✳

TOUGH LOVE

Yet, Christ's mercy is not always gentle. It can be, and often is, tough love: the tiger's love. Christ does not excuse our weakness, does not pat us on the head and tell us that the wrong we have done, the illusions we have built, the lies we have told, are all okay. He does not tell us that these do not matter, or that he will free us from all the consequences of what we have been or done.

Christ will never turn away from us, whatever we do or become, even if we turn away from him; this is the clear teaching of the Christian faith. But it is also clear that Christ will not condone our remaining unreal. He will not allow us to hide in our illusions and pretences but will call us, sometimes even constrain us, to face them and uproot them from our hearts and thus come back to our true reality. He calls us to repent for them.

This does not happen in a single moment; if we saw all of our unreality all at once, it might lead us to despair. Christ's mercy instead leads us to it slowly, step by step. One moment it may be a negative emotion—jealousy, resentment or fear—that has been eating away at our heart but that we had not been able to understand or acknowledge until now. The next moment we are asked to face and to dismantle our pride or egotism or any other of the countless tendencies and feelings that keep us from being true to ourselves.

The work of conversion is painful, difficult and never-ending; we can never finish dismantling our unreality once and for all. The work of conversion is like weeding a garden: we pull the weeds of unreality one day, only to find them popping up again the next. We repeat the same mistake, the same sin, over and over again, for the soil of our soul has been long neglected, ignored and poisoned with fear. We must weed it out again and again. It is a lifetime's work.

No one is exempt from this never-ending "sinning"; there is no one who does not need to ask for mercy and healing of the heart every day. The greatest saints knew that they did. Ceaseless conversion was first taught and practised by men and women of heroic sanctity and love. Surely we cannot claim that we are exempt from it! Only Christ, who was fully, boundlessly real, did not need to repent.

And yet when Christ, as Christians believe, took upon himself the sins of the world—the whole of the world's unreality—he repented for it for the sake of us all. He who "knew no sin" (2 Corinthians 5:21) showed us through his own life and death what dreadful evil human sin and alienation from God brings into the world, and how it must be overcome.

✳

NOT ALONE

*C*hrist took upon himself every aspect of the suffering and alienation that we all must struggle with. He set no limits to what he would do for our sake. He bore the aloneness, the sense of abandonment that torments us at times, the terror of death that sooner or later we must face. He spared himself nothing, not even despair. Christ's last cry on the cross—"Father, why have you abandoned me?"—leaves no doubt in our minds about how far he was prepared to go in his identification with us.

The suffering and death of Christ reveal to us the true meaning of unreality and reveal the price that he paid for it and that we, in our small measure, must pay for it, too. But they also reveal to us the true meaning of death. Christ did not abolish death; he did not take it away from us, for death is the natural end of all finite life. Neither did he take away from us the fear of death that we share with every living creature.

Christ faced this same fear as he lay sweating blood in the Garden, and he had to face it alone, as we all will have to face it one day. For, however greatly we have loved and been loved in life, however closely we are surrounded by family and friends at the end, we always have to face the moment of our death alone. There is no other person—not even the most beloved of friends—who can fully share our death: no one but Christ.

Only Christ can share our fear and our death with us and conquer it in us as he conquered it in himself. By suffering death in its full horror, Christ filled it with his own victory and thus removed its sting. Death, he showed us, however painful and terrifying it may be, is not the end, and we are not alone. Christ abides within our death as fully as he abides within our life and gives it its true meaning. When, shining with the light and glory of heaven, Christ rose from the tomb, he blessed our death and changed it forever. He consecrated it, making it into a meeting place of time and eternity: a mystery-event.

This truth is difficult for us to understand and to embrace. The fear of death is so deeply rooted in us, such an integral part of our human reality, that to face it and try to uproot it may seem too painful, too inhuman to undertake. For it brings us face to face with what we now realize has always been our greatest fear: the fear of mortality, of our own reality marked already with the dissolution of death. It is when we accept this truth about ourselves that we begin to understand the full meaning of mercy and of our unceasing need for it.

We see that to pray for mercy—to repent—is also, as the early Christian teachers taught, a way of preparing ourselves for death. It is our practice of death. By placing ourselves again and again in the presence of Christ and asking for his mercy and love, we participate in his death and make our own death less frightening. We know now how we shall meet it. We shall keep on saying, "Have mercy on me, a sinner!" even with our last breath.

✳

EMPTY HEART

As we continue our work of salvation, as we dismantle layer after layer of our unreality and let go of all that is not true in ourselves, we come at last, perhaps only at the end of our lives, face to face with the reality of who we really are, what we really fear, what we have defended ourselves from for most of our lives. And it is only then that we glimpse the true significance of the "inner room" that Christ called us to enter and where he promised to abide with us.

At the very core of our being, we discover, there is and has always been a secret, empty room, a sacred space for God to fill. There has always been a door to it, a door we could open to find him whom our heart has sought all our lives. Our tragedy has been that in our ignorance we were so often afraid to enter this room because we were terrified of its emptiness; it made us feel separated from others, vulnerable and alone.

And so, we tried to fill this emptiness with many things: with interesting ideas and great pretensions; with possessions, pleasure or fame. We have created a false self for ourselves, a false identity that makes us feel significant. In the end, we may even convince ourselves that there is nothing more to us than the false self we have assumed; we forget our true heart and become meaningless.

But as we continue our work of dismantling all the rubbish we have piled at the door of our inner room, we remember more and more clearly what lies behind it and become less and less afraid of opening it. And, if we persevere in our work, then one day, perhaps only at the end of our lives, we shall find what we have been searching for all these years: our fully healed, fully real, fully loving heart.

And then, with amazement, awe and boundless joy, we may realize that what we have found is not at all what we had expected and even feared to find. It is not some perfect, ideal self that we had imagined we should be and felt guilty for not being. It is not any "self" at all; it is only an empty human heart filled to overflowing by the love of Christ. The emptiness we feared so much is not the emptiness of aloneness, but the emptiness of total openness and freedom.

It is Christ—God within—who is and has always been waiting for us in the empty room at the core of our being. It is Christ who is and always has been the true meaning and purpose of our lives. It is Christ whom we have always loved and searched for. We have found him at last and have become, like Mary, Theotokos herself, "Christ bearers": true icons of Christ. While still on earth, we have already entered the life of Heaven. There has never been anything else for us to seek or hope for, nothing else to find.

✳

Notes

1   Madonna House is a Catholic community of men, women and priests living a life of poverty, chastity and obedience. It was founded by a Russian emigrée, Catherine Kolyschkine-Doherty, in 1947. (Although born and baptized Orthodox, she became a Catholic after her arrival in the West in 1919.) She came to Combermere, Ontario, with her husband Edward Doherty after spending 20 years living with the poor and serving them, first in Toronto and then in Chicago and Harlem. She was also one of the pioneers of the civil rights movement in the United States.

At the present time, the Community has about 200 members, about half of them living in Combermere, where the main training centre is located. Others live in 20 "field houses" in Canada, the United States, the West Indies, England, Belgium, Russia and Africa. The work of the Community lies principally in being available to all who come to one of their houses and offering them hospitality, prayers and, above all, acceptance and love. In two or three bigger houses, meals are served to the homeless and donated clothes are distributed.

Catherine Doherty died in 1985 in Combermere at the age of 89. She was the author of many books, of which *Poustinia* (a Russian word for *desert*) is perhaps the best known. Her full biography, *They Called Her the Baroness*, by Lorene Hanley Duquin, was published by Alba Press, New York, in 1995.

2   The Jesus Prayer has been compared to the "just sitting" and watching one's breath of Zen. Like Zen meditation, the Jesus Prayer is a way of waking up to reality: to what is really there. This comparison, however, should not be pushed too far. In the

139

Christian tradition, Christ can never be viewed simply as a focus of attention, a way to help us become more aware of reality. He *is* the reality we seek. The Jesus Prayer is above all a *prayer*.

3   A Monk of the Eastern Church (Lev Gillet), *The Jesus Prayer* (Crestwood, NY: St. Vladimir's Seminary Press, 1987).

4   Joseph Raya, Retired Archbishop of Galilee, d. 2005 at Madonna House.

5   Human beings of all religious traditions have always recognized the presence of the divine in the natural world. They saw it especially clearly in many holy sites, where they believed it could be encountered more easily. As my daughter, Kathryn Zaleski-Cox, pointed out to me, the ancient (pre-Christian) Irish called such sites "thin places," where the wall between the earthly reality and the divine appeared to be especially transparent. Many of these places were later "baptized" and are even now revered as holy places dedicated to various Irish saints.

6   Mother Maria, *Eastern Spirituality* (Toronto: Peregrina Press, 1992), p. 11. (First published in 1973.) See also Irma Zaleski, *Encounters with the Desert Mother* (Toronto: Peregrina Press, 2001), pp. 58–59.

7   I owe the inspiration for this chapter to an interesting talk (as yet unpublished) by Fr. Kevin Flynn of Saint Paul University on "Yoga and a Sacramental World View."

8   The present English version of the Nicene Creed recited at Mass states that the Word "became man," wording that seems to obscure the true meaning of the Mystery. The original version did not say "man" or even a "body," but *flesh*. My theologian brother informs me that the present wording was "an oversight" and that the next version will correct it. This, if it comes, would seem to me to be a necessary correction: not primarily because the present version is not inclusive (although that is a problem

for many as well), but because it undermines the essential meaning of the Christian proclamation.

9 In the Eastern Christian tradition, Christ is believed to have been born in a cave, and most modern scholars agree that this is most likely. The sheep were often herded for the night in caves, where the shepherds could best guard them.

10 It is worth noting that they also believed that, at the end of time, not only our bodies but the whole of reality would be radically transformed, that "there will be a new heaven and a new earth" (Revelation 21:1). (I find it very interesting that, in the same verse, we are also told that "the sea will be no more." The sea for the Hebrews was an image of danger and primeval chaos. There is no place for either in the redeemed creation. From this perspective, we can understand why Christ's walking on the water was such a powerful sign of Christ's eternal lordship.)

11 I mention this dream not because I view dreams (my own or those reported to me by my friends) as "inspired" or necessarily of any general significance. But I have learned that dreams can be very helpful in understanding what is going on in ourselves, what we are really feeling or struggling with.

12 Mother Maria Gysi, in a short essay on the Trinity in *The Fool and Other Writings* (Normaby, Whitby, UK: Greek Orthodox Monastery of the Assumption, 1980), p. 57. See also the *Catechism of the Catholic Church* (no. 170). This is why, perhaps, the Eastern Church rarely talks of the doctrines of Christianity as dogmas but refers to them as mysteries. They are not to be explained or too quickly defined, but proclaimed, reflected upon and approached with wonder and awe. As Gregory of Nyssa said in the fourth century, "God is not to be named, but to be wondered at."

13 The only exceptions are a few well-known friendships between men and women of great holiness (and chastity). St. Francis of Assisi and St. Claire, Teresa of Avilla and John of the Cross, Francis de Sales and Jeanne de Chantal are among the best known. In our own time, perhaps the most notable example is the friendship of Hans Urs von Balthasar and Adrienne von Speyr.

14 It is difficult to see why it is marital love, the union of a man and a woman in marriage, that became nearly exclusively the image of the love between Christ and a Christian "soul." In his parables, Christ used the image of bridegroom and bride to indicate his relationship with the Church, but nowhere in the four canonical Gospels does he compare his love for any of his disciples to the love of a husband for his spouse. He calls them his "friends." (Note, however, that the image of "bridal" love between Christ and the soul is central in the uncanonical Gospel of Philip, which the early Church either did not know or knew and rejected as "gnosticism.") It may also be interesting to note that Aelred, the English twelfth-century monk and writer, is reported to have said that "God is Friendship," thus rephrasing St. John's statement that God is Love.

15 I write of this experience (as well as of my memories of Dante) with Renee's knowledge and permission.

16 Since I wrote this chapter, I came across D. M. Dooling's article "The Fire Proveth Iron," in *The Inner Journey: Views in the Christian Tradition* (Sandpoint, ID: Morning Light Press, 2006, pp. 85–86; reprinted from *Parabola Magazine*, vol. 10, no. 4). Dooley writes, "Evil is…a willed, because consented-to disintegration…. Joined with the human will, it becomes a force, although in itself it is really nothing." She adds this quotation from St. Augustine's *Confessions:* "I inquired what iniquity was and found it to be no substance but a perversion of the will turned aside from…God" (Book 7, XVI).

17 A friend who had spent some time at a Trappist monastery told me a story that illustrates this point. There was a monk there who had impressed my friend with his kindness and humility. When my friend was leaving the monastery, he went to say goodbye to the monk and decided to tell him of this impression. The monk thanked him and then said, "It is a strange thing that God sends us enemies to teach us humility but friends to make us proud again!" I used this story in *Mother Macrina* (Ottawa: Novalis, 2001, p. 69).

18 The two paragraphs on John the Baptist are taken from my article "Forerunner of Truth" in *Parabola, Magazine of Myth and Tradition*, Fall 2000 issue, p. 47.

19 The word *conversion* comes from the Latin *conversio*, which literally means a *turning back*. As the *Dictionary of the New Testament* points out, "The English terms 'conversion' and 'turning back' are preferred to the word repentance which suggests a penalty for a fault to be 'repented of'; an idea that is inadequate for expressing the radical transformation of one's being and the fruits of conversion." (*Dictionary of the New Testament* by Xavier Leon-Dufour, tr. from the French by Terence Prendergast, p. 146). I reflected on this fundamental Christian insight more fully in *Conversion of the Heart: The Way of Repentance* (Ottawa: Novalis, 2003).